Pastor's Handbook on Interpersonal Relationships

Keys to Successful Leadership

Jard DeVille

BAKER BOOK HOUSE
Grand Rapids, Michigan 49506

Contents

List of Illustrations

Preface

There is no doubt in my mind that pastors—who struggle daily against the world's sin and evil, ignorance, fears, and stagnant complacency—are the unsung heroes of the church of the Lord Jesus Christ. They labor long hours (often for salaries no self-respecting plumber would accept), use skills that would serve them well in a management team or professional counseling practice, and are "on call" so continually that their personal lives and the interests of their families must usually settle for second place. To make matters worse, they frequently must do their jobs without the wholehearted support of their congregations, riddled as they often are with divisive conflict and cross-purposes. In fact, it has been said that the church is the only army that shoots its wounded leaders.

Christian leadership is obviously quite different from management in the secular sphere, despite some elements of similarity. In contrast to other institutions, the church does much of its hands-on labor through the efforts of unpaid workers and faces all the limitations on power and control that a volunteer arrangement implies. The pastor of a congregation faces the unique challenge of implementing overall goals by offering mainly intangible rewards, the importance of which is often ignored by captains of industry. What a minister has to offer fellow workers in Christ's vineyard is not a pay raise, extra holidays, or prestigious promotions for diligent efforts, but a

13

richer way of life—a better way to feel about one's relationship with God, with neighbors, and with oneself.

Although that is powerful motivation indeed, a parish leader must still communicate his or her own personal commitment in such a way that the Christian lifestyle becomes meaningful and rewarding to the parishioners. This is no easy assignment in today's congregations, which are often made up of people with differing backgrounds, interests, and economic levels. Nor is it made simpler by living in a technological society where material goals and conflicting standards of ethics are so openly dangled before the world's humanity.

No longer can a minister be merely a model of piety and quiet contemplation or a sound teacher of theological principles. A successful parish leader must excel in persuasion techniques by offering some rather sophisticated psychospiritual rewards. He or she must begin where the people are—by understanding and activating the basic principles of human psychology—and then lead the membership in activities that many of their neighbors find puzzling.

Successful congregational leadership harnesses the physical, mental, and spiritual talents within the parish, so that people increasingly find personal redemption and ongoing sanctification in Christ-exemplified lifestyles. Only when there is consistent maturation in discipleship can individuals transcend the tragic triad of suffering, guilt, and death that visits everyone at one time or another. When personal commitment is shared and further strengthened by the cohesiveness and unified purpose available in a fellowship of believers, Christianity can truly become a vital force for good in the community at large.

What best characterizes a successful parish leader? Why are good ones so hard to come by? The answer to the first question explains the second. No matter how well-intentioned a minister may be in his or her efforts to guide, teach, counsel, and demonstrate Christian principles to the membership, the efforts reap a limited harvest if the sower fails to realize that the key to a successful parish leadership lies with interpersonal relationships. Without a knowledge of how humans are motivated and interact with one another, and the flexibility to apply "people skills" appropriately, no minister or lay-leader can be truly effective. When sound relationships are missing, people will be unenthusiastic or negative about even the most worthwhile programs. Therein lies the cause of stunted growth for many congregations, which either smother in useless busy work or stagnate for lack of direction. It is only as a parish leader draws on interpersonal strengths that desired response is reinforced and thriving congregations are built and growth sustained.

Some years ago I was in one of the last workshops led by Hiam Ginott. This earthy Israeli psychologist let his superb Jewish humor and logic shine as he taught a group of clinic directors. Eventually someone asked whether Ginott could actually name anyone who had found lasting satisfaction by using interpersonal skills in a leadership setting.

Ginott thought for a few minutes and then to our surprise named Jesus as an example. That set us back on our heels, and one woman protested. She said that many people would think that example unfair, since—after all—Jesus was considered by millions to be God Incarnate and thus more than just a pretty effective itinerant preacher. Did Ginott know of anyone else?

After a little more reflection, our workshop leader named a tentmaker from Tarsus by the name of Saul. He was, Ginott explained, so caught up in his cause that he probably found self-actualization through his work and relationships. We digested that for a while until someone else said that Paul might also be considered a bit of a heavy-hitter for those of us who merely wanted to manage our clinics well and had no aspiration for martyred sainthood. Name an ordinary person, we asked—one with the kinds of fears and pressures we face today, someone with whom we could identify.

Ginott scratched his head for a moment and came up with another shocker, this time another field preacher, though from England not Palestine. This leader, he said, used every bit of the knowledge and wisdom of his time to exercise true leadership. He worked through the poor people of his country in a very class-conscious era and changed the very history of the church. This chap was John Wesley, explained Ginott with a grin—a man who knew what he wanted and knew how to lead people to work with him toward that goal.

Since our aircraft were soon to leave in different directions, I had no time to explore the Israeli's fascination with Christian leaders. It would have been fascinating to learn why he decided that Jesus, Paul, and John Wesley had lived deeply fulfilling lives. It obviously mattered not to Ginott that each died penniless, though rich in intangible rewards. Wesley's legacy, for example, was a worn-out suit of clothes, a spavined old nag, a battered Bible—*and* the Methodist Church! Not too shabby an epitaph for a wandering preacher!

I believe that only the great fellowship of the redeemed has the insights and strengths needed to act as leaven in society. The church—the light of the world, the city set upon a hill, the branches of the living vine—is the only one of all the world's institutions making a concerted effort to transcend the narrow secular values and nihilistic pessimism that threaten to destroy humankind. Yet here, too, the church sometimes fails in its ministry because of human shortcomings.

Christians are given spiritual treasures in earthen vessels, and sometimes the pots are misshapen, improperly fired, or even cracked! Too many Christians cling to a vested interest in some physical, psychological, or philosophical status quo and do not take kindly to a pastor who calls them to mature discipleship. One has only to preach about the dangers of building nuclear weapons to a congregation whose jobs depend on military spending to be soundly condemned by those whose ox you gored. Or try discussing the ethics of growing tobacco with the farmers of North Carolina!

Yet we all know strong pastoral leaders who work with and through their congregations to accomplish spectacular things for God and his people. Within a few miles of my home there are several such pastors in action. They work in five different denominations and many social settings—ranging from Phil Hinerman's inner-city multi-racial congregation to Art Rouner's ministry in the most exclusive suburb of Minneapolis. The city church hires fifty workers to oversee its summer youth program, and the suburban parish gives tens of thousands of dollars annually to African relief.

What about the people in the pews of *your* church? Are they growing in spiritual maturity, making a difference as true disciples? Too often, congregations must wait too long—or in vain— for the kind of leadership that will capture their enthusiasm, unleash their untapped abilities, and direct their energy toward creative service that will help them fulfill their own spiritual goals as well.

The purpose of this book is to help you, their pastoral leader, master interpersonal relationships so as to become the best you can be—for God, for his people, and for yourself!

Jard DeVille, PhD.

PART I

Relationships and Leadership

I

Understanding Leadership

I will go on record right here to report that working as a leadership consultant in the Judeo-Christian tradition is an ancient and honorable profession. It goes back to the time of Moses, who retained his more experienced father-in-law, Jethro, to investigate what was going wrong in his congregation. Jethro did his research, at a reputed 500-silver-shekels per day plus camel expenses, and identified Moses' first leadership problem. Jethro's report comes down to us verbatim:

> Now let me give you some good advice, and God will be with you. It is right for you to represent the people before God and bring their disputes to him. You should teach them God's commands and explain to them how they should live and what they should do. But in addition, you should choose some capable men and appoint them as leaders of the people: leaders of thousands, hundreds, fifties, and tens. They must be God-fearing men who can be trusted and who cannot be bribed. Let them serve as judges for the people on a permanent basis. They can bring all the difficult cases to you, but they themselves can decide all the smaller disputes. That will make it easier for you, as they share your burden.
> Exodus 18:19–22

A short time ago I was conducting a pastoral-leadership workshop for a group of clergy in a western city. I asked the participants to share their concepts of leadership as it applies to a local congregation. To keep them on their toes, I restricted their definitions to no more than a few words.

21

The men and women in the seminar soon filled my flip chart with such terms as "delegation," "motivation," "control," "persuasion," and "managing." Finally one last word was offered, and the group collectively let out a sigh, for we knew intuitively that it was the one term we wanted. The word was *influence*. As we focused on the concept, the group hammered out this definition for parish leadership:

> Pastoral leadership is the continuous process by which a minister tries to influence the members' attitudes and actions in order to reach specific goals.

Elements of Leadership Influence

This definition of leadership has some important implications. In the first place, leadership emerges as an ongoing, planned activity within the parish. Although certain people regularly fill formal and informal leadership positions, leadership implies that there is also a group of followers who more or less consistently look to the leader(s) for guidance. Finally, the activities of both leaders and followers are directed deliberately toward the completion of certain tasks. Leadership thereby implies a goal-directed process.

It soon becomes obvious that considerable leadership may be exercised in a parish by someone other than the formal, titular head of the congregation. Here is one example, from the viewpoint of a lay person:

> Our pastor is Dr. Wheatly. He looks after everything, does most of the preaching, administers the staff's work, and is very succesful at raising money. But Carl and Anne are the real spark plugs with the congregation. They direct the witnessing and evangelism programs, find leaders for the Bible studies, work with youth groups, set up our mini-churches of ten families each, and do everything else that wins new people to the church. Dr. Wheatly's work is vital, but it's the two kids who keep the pots bubbling.

When I talked to the senior pastor, Dr. Wheatly let me know

that it was no accident that he had chosen the two young associates. He said:

> Of course they do what I can't. We've had a serious financial challenge because our membership has doubled without many of the new families learning to tithe yet. And little would happen without the funds I raise. I saw the need for Carl and Anne, which is why I recruited them. They'll not stay long, for some other congregation will call them to pastorates of their own. But I'm certainly making the most use of them while I can.

Dr. Wheatly must have read Jethro's advice to Moses! There was no doubt he had multiplied his wisdom and effectiveness through a pair of fine young people.

The influence that one uses in leading a congregation is always associated closely with power and prestige, both of which come from a variety of sources within the organization. For, despite the fact that the church is of God, it always remains a cultural association made up of individuals and small groups, all with interests, needs, and activities that must be coordinated. The church, in other words, never ceases to be a human organization with all the values, attitudes, and expectations of its members caught in a cultural whirlwind.

When Dr. Wheatly works with bankers to raise the money needed to build a new educational unit, his power to negotiate comes largely from his position as the formal head of a large, still-growing church in the community. Local financiers listen because the pastor has proven money-management ability and controls a certain amount of financial power within his congregation. When, on the other hand, Anne and Carl work successfully with groups of teenagers, they influence the young people largely through their interpersonal know-how. There is a difference in goals, methods, tools, and abilities, but both approaches are vital in congregational leadership.

As a result of my research throughout different denominations and congregations, I have identified four basic types of pastoral power. A minister must learn when each is appropriate, if he or she hopes to influence others—to motivate them toward constructive goals without causing damaging aftereffects.

Position Power. The senior minister is the titular head of the parish. The degree of position power will vary in different kinds of churches, of course. For example, a Catholic priest holds authority that comes directly from the Pope and thus has considerable job security that few Baptist ministers can claim. The latter are typically hired and fired at the pleasure of the local congregation. In some denominations, the minister must even survive an official annual challenge to remain in office. In any case, position power is a major source of influence in any congregation that is serious about reaching out in Christ's name.

Coercion Power. Herein is reflected the ability of a pastor or a board to punish people. In our time and place, however, few ministers have a great deal of this type of power unless the congregation delegates it to them. There are simply too many other congregations and denominations in which people are welcome. Most coercive power comes out of a belief that one's own denomination and/or congregation is the only one acceptable to God. Belonging to the one "true" denomination can be a strong influence for people who do not understand anything about the individual priesthood of believers—or about Christ as Advocate for each Christian. Except in the cults—which work largely from motives other than the maturation of their members, as did James Jones of Jonestown—most pastors have little coercion power.

A dear friend of mine discovered the limits of his, early in his ministry. Charles Watson is a mellow pastor now, but as a young man he tried to coerce a couple who had challenged him on a point made in his Sunday sermon. What right, they asked, did he have to say such a thing when it was not to be found in the Scriptures? Charles chuckles tolerantly now as he relates the story. He tells how he pointed to his clerical collar, just as his old Dutch pastor did when Charles was a youngster. He growled in his most authoritarian manner that *it* was all the justification he needed. The young husband stood up, told the pastor how to handle his collar, and led his wife from the office. The following Sunday, Charles looked up from bidding communicants goodbye to see the young couple entering another church across the street. He never did get them back!

Reinforcement Power. This type of influence comes from the ability to offer rewards that people want. Praise, public affirmation, scrolls, and attendance pins can be used to move men and women toward a desired course of action. Praise, however, must be used as sparingly and wisely as a physician uses a strong medicine. Indiscriminate use soon causes it to lose its effect. I know a pastor who smiles continually, claps everyone on the shoulder, and mutters "Atta boy! [or Atta girl!]" over and over until everyone simply tunes him out. His excessive use of praise has become meaningless.

I once felt the same way about those little pins and bars given for Sunday-school attendance. No matter how I tried, I could never make it through the full year—often because some kid who had no business in Sunday school had given *me* the flu or a bad cold the previous week! In fact, the pins even became a disincentive to me, because I soon began to ask myself, "What's another absence when I can't win?" Such material rewards can help, however, in some situations.

Rewards must be proportional to the value of the service given, must be offered at the right time, and should always be withheld if the service is done badly. Nevertheless, reinforcement power can be very effective for a perceptive pastor, as I will explain later.

Performance Power. Here the potential power is derived from the skills, knowledge, and wisdom brought to bear by the minister on the needs of the congregation. This is doubtless the most useful source of power in a volunteer organization such as the local congregation. A powerful pulpit preacher will surely influence people more strongly than a weak speaker who presents the same ideas and illustrations in a less effective manner. Most performance power, of course, normally comes from setting good examples.

I recently heard Robert Schuller lecturing to a group of ministers at a conference. We had all been buzzing around, greeting old friends and making new ones. The MC's introduction was uninspiring, and we were tired because the day had been filled with workshop activities. Yet, when Pastor Schuller began to speak in his soft, low key manner, we listened carefully. There was no restless shifting of chairs, no murmuring, not even a nervous cough to be heard. The audience became so quiet that you could have heard a mouse crossing the floor. Because of the man's performance power and resultant influence, he had everyone's attention. The power of his example was indisputable.

Channeling Leadership Power

The four common sources of pastoral power, apart from that which comes from God as a spiritual source, fall into two logical categories. Position power and coercion power, delegated to the minister by the denomination and congregation, create the pastor's *authoritative influence* over the people. On the other hand, the use of reinforcement power and performance power form his or her *achievement influence,* the other half of the balance. Once more, the volunteer relationship between pastor and people puts this in a fragile setting. The pastor must work with a sophistication seldom seen in military, business, industrial, and governmental organizations, since these generally emphasize strong authoritarian and coercive power over their members. Unfortunately, as in the case of my friend Charles, it takes time and often several serious failures to learn this fact of life in the ministry. Some clergy never do, so they go through life unsuccessfully ministering to dwindling congregations that turn inward with inordinate pride in their spirituality. It is all too common to rationalize one's failure by blaming someone else. Some pastors and congregations do so by assuming a mantle of excessive purity and spirituality, claiming that they live with greater devotion to God—with deeper piety than those "unspiritual" people who compromised with the world for greater growth. What a tragedy to feel that way!

Although each congregation works within its own house style and subculture in the local community, every successful church I have seen uses a leadership approach whose elements are diagrammed in figure 1. This method channels the authoritative/ achievement influences—the power mechanisms—in such a way that they are maximized in the interrelated and ongoing processes of planning, implementing, assessing, and rewarding. The stated aim may be to achieve specific performance "results" so as to reach interim and final goals, but of equal importance is evoking a positive response in all participants. This more subtle and psychological end is desirable in itself, and it can also be a valuable resource to be drawn upon for church solidarity and future problem solving. Ironically, most of these principles evolved from secular "management programs," although they have considerable relevance for church leadership as well.

 **Channeling Influence**

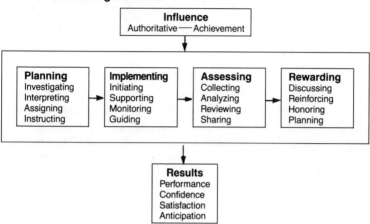

A brief illustration may clarify how this works. Not very long ago I consulted with a pastor named Philip Anderson. It was his intention to develop an evangelism program that made use of my book *Psychology of Witnessing*. With a team of callers as the immediate goal, he and I spent some time discussing his resources and opportunities before developing a growth strategy.

Planning. After I left, Phil used his authoritative achievement influence to plan the program in its initial stages. Almost immediately after that, my client brought in the key lay-leaders of the congregation, set them to defining subgoals, planning the details, and accepting the responsibility and rewards of the evangelism effort. A committee was formed to coordinate the actual outreach in the community, with the pastor and lay-leaders to be very visible and regularly active.

Because Phil was a little leery of committees that fizzle and founder, he called the group the Evangelism Task Force. That, he told me, shifted the emphasis from discussion to action. Be careful, however, not to reject the concept of the much-maligned "committee." If it is well led and made up of committed members, it is the unit that will do most of the work. When properly persuaded and influenced by a hard-working committee, people will give their best for Christ and the church, offering their greatest efforts. Use the task force, as my friend did, to spread the effort through the rest of the congregation. In this case, the aim was to develop teams of people to call and witness, with the members of the task force serving as small-team leaders.

Phil used the study-guide portion of *Psychology of Witnessing* to train his members in what and how to persuade others to consider a Christian commitment. Even as the organization of the calling teams and their training was beginning, some of the task-force members were conducting a feasibility study on how to use the teams most effectively. Information was gathered and the data interpreted by the pastor and his key lay-leaders. There was little argument about the results of the investigation, since the two major areas in which to work included one that was filled with people who had bought their homes and reared their children shortly after World War II. The other area, on the opposite side of the community, was filled with housing tracts teeming with a mini-babyboom. Phil chose to concentrate on the kids, of course. Outreach volunteers were briefed on effective witnessing techniques and general area assignments were made.

Implementing. The overall action plan began with a door-to-door survey, a method I learned from Elwood Munger almost a generation ago. Members of the witnessing group stopped at every home where there were indications of children, identified themselves to the parents, offered the children trinkets to catch their attention, and offered to take the kids to a forthcoming Sunday-school rally by church bus. There was usually no need to explain at this time that the "church bus" was a family car, driven by the caller to collect children in the assigned area. As planned, it was hoped that the kids would draw the parents into the church orbit.

Implementation always draws strongly on people resources. Men and women began witnessing to friends and neighbors, knocking on doors, driving their cars, burning their own fuel, looking after the kids, teaching classes and Bible studies. Each worker was expected to keep in close contact with the children and their parents, monitoring progress and offering personalized support and guidance when called for.

Assessing. Evaluation is given a formal place in the system but early feedback must always occur. As progress was periodically reviewed, several problems were discovered in the neighborhood calling and witnessing. One of the team captains stumbled badly and had to be replaced. Another team needed additional training in the Munger Method and so on. Fortunately, I had explained to Phil in advance that he should expect to make mid-course adjustments in order to win the best results. The problems did discourage him for a while, but he went on and soon found a realizable goal in sight—contact with a strong group of new families with which to build his congregation.

Rewarding. It is obvious that this stage of the action plan overlaps the other three in varying degrees. Progress toward a sound goal depends on inherent, ongoing rewards for all participants. Team captains and the overall "chairperson"—in this case, Phil—periodically interact with the hands-on workers, providing reinforcement for specific achievements, encouragement as individual problems arise, and opportunities for discussing the foreseen results, now recognized as soon-to-be realized. As progress reports are shared, new ideas emerge for reaching the defined goal.

In Phil's case, after the work had been done, an awards dinner was held in the church fellowship hall. Workers were honored with praise, scrolls, and plaques. It is all very well to say that God provides spiritual rewards for faithful stewards, but it also helps a great deal to add a few human strokes by fellow workers in the here and now. Like a powerful medicine, appropriate praise and tangible rewards for a job well done can accomplish miracles, if the affirmation comes from leaders we trust, love, and respect.

Results. Here it is assumed that the original goal has been met. As concrete data are documented and performance affirmed, the confidence level of all concerned is generally high. Satisfaction in one joint venture can foster anticipation of concerted efforts ahead, especially as ideas for related projects have emerged during the plan's execution.

Phil's witnessing program started somewhat more than a year ago, and his congregation has now grown to a point where the membership has had to call for an associate pastor. This marks real achievement, since an average of only two out of ten congregations ever grow to a size where they can afford more than one minister. *Note:* For further details about how to conduct a successful local evangelism program, see chapter sixteen.

Leadership Structures

The leadership methods and style needed by a growing congregation are never static. Leadership is always a fluid activity, especially in a new congregation assembling as a community need or in a spin-off group from an already-successful fellowship. Grace Church—An Evangelical Fellowship, located in a Minneapolis suburb—has already formed two satellite congregations and is not ready to stop yet. Such a new congregation always needs a strong pastor who has a compelling need to bring people into a personal relationship with Christ and/or a desire to succeed in his or her own calling. This is certainly a legitimate combination, since I cannot believe that God calls ministers to failure.

A mission congregation works through relationships that are invariably as simple and direct as humanly possible. Such a church simply does not have the luxuries of large salaries, generous equipment budgets, and outreach organizations. Personal commitment is all-important. Everyone knows each other, relates personally and intimately, and generally feels the need to give support and help wherever needed. Great things can be accomplished in this age-old manner. Yet, the successes such congregations have, often growing from one hundred to two hundred members in one year, create the need for a more formal and sometimes complex governance structure. This often requires both a more formal pastor than the original builder of the mission congregation and more scientific management practices for emerging lay-leaders.

The Pyramid. If Jethro's advice is followed, associate ministers and lay administrators are hired to oversee the music, the youth programs, and the ongoing evangelism. The new surge of growth can be created and sustained for a while—right up to the point where the members begin to feel as if they are lost in the machinery of worship and service. It is in such a manner that many congregations peak on their own growth. Certainly the average degree of commitment can decline when the leadership pyramid expands and clogs the avenues of communication.

Not long ago in a distant city, I attended the morning worship service of such a church with my daughter. Although we listened and participated appropriately, when it was over she turned to me and said, "This is a factory, and the product they turn out is mass worship."

She was right. Any church needs a better approach to leadership when a large membership is reached, if it hopes to mature past the double plateau of a normal progression. The congregation must develop beyond the entrepreneur stage to a meaningful division of labor, as Jethro counseled Moses. Then it must move ahead to become a fully functioning, self-directing spiritual community of men and women who are committed to Christ, to the church, and to each other. Obviously, a church that reaches a scientific-management middle stage does not become a unified spiritual community by simply wanting that goal. It must make the challenging and sometimes expensive choices that lead to another stage of growth. It must mature beyond the traditional business-and-industry pyramid of control and leadership.

It is all very well for such denominations as the Roman Catholic Church and the United Methodist Church to appoint or elect bishops to power, giving them authority over the pastors. However, the almost-inevitable result is to reward the pastors who avoid making waves and penalize those who depart from the official line. Unfortunately, very few entrepreneur pastors will emerge from such a system. In any case, the hierarchical system breaks down as you work past the professional pastors in the succession to deal with the people in the pews. Then leadership influence becomes paramount.

I have always found it significant that the Roman Catholic Church has prospered for two thousand years with only three levels in its hierarchy. With this pyramid, no one is ever far removed from the lines of communication and command. That is something one cannot say about a great many government and business organizations, which have a steep pyramid with many levels rather than the broad, shallow one that describes Catholic hierarchy. There is, however, a far better structure for use in a volunteer organization such as the local congregation. This "cloverleaf" approach lends itself to greater influence and a faster reaction time. It makes the most of leadership that is based on example and achievement rather than on authority.

The Cloverleaf. This leadership structure maximizes the communication that flows between pastor and people in both

Figure 2 **Cloverleaf Leadership**

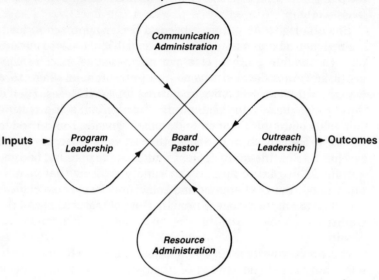

directions, the setting of goals and objectives by the members themselves, the "ownership" of the church's responsibilities and rewards, and member self-direction. Obviously, when a good percentage of the members of a congregation serve God and the fellowship in this manner, success shall certainly follow. The people begin to accept certain missions for themselves and can evaluate their success in reaching their objectives. The cloverleaf that can effectively replace congregational pyramids is shown in figure 2.

In this leadership approach, the church board and the pastor are centered and activities swirl around them. This hub is where the streams of communication, resources, and efforts meet and cross. In my consulting, I generally advise clients to begin by dealing with resource administration, lest one find the congregation running short of the materials with which to work. Here one is reminded of the biblical case of the builder who began to raise a high tower without counting the cost. He eventually abandoned the project at great personal loss and humiliation. I have seen churches do just that—starting, for example, a mission congregation, by building a basement church with the intention of completing the sanctuary later. Without adequate forethought, well-intentioned planners can lose their vision, and the project remains underground for decades.

After considering the resources available and how they are to be managed, program leadership is needed to harness the strengths of individuals in specific projects and missions. Effective management of communications can keep the people marching generally to the same drummer, although it is both inevitable and wise to encourage many different missions under the umbrella of the church. Finally, outreach leadership is extended into the community at large to persuade men and women to come to Christ and find lasting fellowship in a growing, maturing community of Christians. This brings the leadership/administrative process full circle to the need for additional resources in order to continue the growth cycle. There must be continual input of ideas and material assets to sustain the health of the congregation.

Balancing Resources and Relationships

As you can see by looking at the cloverleaf diagram, two of the task loops deal with inanimate administration, while the others are about interpersonal leadership. I developed this approach in my recent book *The Psychology of Leadership,* where I reported that anyone responsible for the productivity of an organization has two areas through which to succeed. First is the "hardware" of administration—the resources with which to prosper. Second, a good manager must also deal with the "software" of leadership—the people who use the resources. Some ministers are better at administering resources while others are better at interpersonal leadership. Both are important and must be mastered in order to succeed. Figure 3 represents an appropriate design for achieving the necessary balance within a congregation.

Richard the Lionhearted, king of England after the Norman Conquest, was a terrible administrator of resources. He was so impatient and restless that he frequently moved several times from pew to pew during the course of a sermon by his chaplain. He could so seldom coordinate the supply wagons and his crusaders that the soldiers marched hungry much of the time.

FIGURE 3 **Balancing Resources and Relationships**

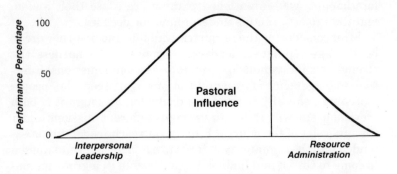

On the other hand, he was such a charismatic leader that men of military age flocked to follow him to Palestine.

Every pastor has to deal with budgets, air-conditioning plants, educational materials, transportation vehicles, and all the rest needed by a congregation. But no one, so far as I have ever heard, was ever inspired to greatness in discipleship because the furnace worked well. Or because the church bus was serviced regularly! Admittedly, it would have been difficult had the heating system malfunctioned on Sunday mornings in January, at least in Minneapolis! But something more is required when it comes to influencing men and women to service.

One of the greatest social changes I find occurring in the English-speaking world, one that increases the difficulty of leading a congregation successfully, is a growing sense of independence among people. Even in the church, men and women have learned that they are not merely automatons to be put to work until they malfunction like a bad generator. Neither can people be considered inventory to be used without regard for their emotions and needs. Humans are highly individualistic, emotional, sometimes fearful and anxious. They are also brave and joyous, creative and independent beings who live in a largely subjective world. To reach out and win the loyal enthusiasm of such as these opens the door for greater success than one would first believe possible.

A great many Christians no longer believe that pastors, teachers, police, politicians, and managers in general know what is best for them. Contemporary church members may say the right things to be polite and avoid confrontation, but no pastor, unless he has brainwashed the people like a cult leader, can lead his congregation around by their respective noses. Even the Roman Catholic Pope has discovered this. He comes to the United States and Canada, preaches stern injunctions about the sin of artificial birth control, and is honored and applauded by the multitudes as a great religious leader—and then 90 percent of English, Canadian, American, and Australasian Catholics of childbearing age go home to use proscribed methods of contraception! It must be very frustrating to the man to have the people differentiate sharply between his authoritative/achievement influence and their own lifestyle. Many women of the world love John Paul II, but they refuse to accept his authority in this very personal area of daily living.

The same is true with the Religious Right in the United States. A great many young people support candidates for office who speak out for the fundamentalist beliefs taught by many pastors. They want to see a restoration of entrepreneurship, the decline of big government, and a rebirth of American influence in the world. But great numbers refuse to support a regression in civil rights, a return to traditional gender limitations, the cessation of environmental protection, and social security. During the lifetime of anyone old enough to read this book, we can expect congregations of men and women who pick and choose for themselves the values, attitudes, and expectations they will hold. At no time should those delegated to church leadership lose sight of this cultural axiom.

Ten Key Factors in Pastoral Leadership

I have recently completed a survey of some highly successful pastors. During our hours of discussion and study, virtually every one of them touched upon almost all of the following aspects of a successful ministry. Learn them, for we shall be returning to them regularly in the rest of this book. No attempt has been made to place them in a hierarchy of importance except for the first suggestion.

1. *Pastors must capture the vision that God has indeed called them to oversee the work of the living Christ.* Get your theology straight: Christ is Redeemer, Sanctifier, and Healer of men and

women who make a personal commitment as they struggle for wholeness in this era of incessant change and confusion.

2. *Offer to the people a new life that transcends the pain and perplexities of a secular, nihilistic, anti-spiritual lifestyle.* Teach, in a multitude of ways, that Christ does offer personal healing in the congregation and works through the relationships we have, both in the church and our personal lives.

3. *Build your own life around spiritual values, positive attitudes, high expectations, mature beliefs, and responsible choices.* It is completely acceptable for you to become successful in life, so never rationalize and accept failure as God's will for your ministry.

4. *Build a community of faith, hope, and love, so strong that many men and women find it deeply satisfying to belong in it.* Work through a series of programs until you discover what succeeds in your congregation, which has its own house style. Then follow through with perception and hard work.

5. *Even if it sounds paradoxical for a strong parish leader, lovingly serve the congregation as God's servant.* Continually invest your life in the lives of the people, even as you stand on the highest hill to call them from their sins and toward acceptance of greater responsibility.

6. *Rid yourself of the idea that the ministry is a life of quiet contemplation and meditation.* The parish is a battleground thickly interspersed with land mines that leave people wounded and dying unless they are wisely led.

7. *Develop strong relationships with people who are especially talented and accustomed to taking the initiative in life and work.* Go where the up-and-coming physicians, teachers, and business managers are. Press upon them the call to invest their lives in something really great—God's work. (Of course, this does not mean neglecting other members, whose skills may be less obvious.)

8. *Be your own best example of the Christian life as you lead the leaders and teach the teachers in the congregation.* Set the example through excellence in preaching, in counseling, and in interpersonal relationships, so that lay-leaders, staff members, and parishioners will want to emulate what makes you outstanding.

9. *Develop an ever-increasingly complex, multi-layered pro-*

*gram to meet the needs of people as more of them enter the con-
gregation.* Identify and utilize the strengths of newcomers as
you develop the kinds of programs they will be willing to lead
and support.

10. *Remain in place long enough to make a real difference in
the life of the parish.* Turning sinners into lifelong disciples of
Christ is a long-term process. Give God a chance to use you
consistently and bring you to greatness; commit yourself to God
rather than to a successful career.

A congregation can succeed rather quickly under wise and
strong leadership. By learning as much as you possibly can
about human personality, motivation, competition, cooperation,
and satisfaction, you can develop your leadership potential and
channel your management skills so as to become an outstanding
pastor.

2

Practicing Leadership

The apostle Paul, no less than Jethro, served the leadership of the early church in what can be called a consultant capacity. He wrote the following to a young pastor:

> This is a true saying: If a man is eager to be a church leader, he desires an excellent work. A church leader must be without fault; he must have only one wife, be sober, self-controlled, and orderly; he must welcome strangers in his home; he must be able to teach; he must not be a drunkard or a violent man, but gentle and peaceful; he must not love money; he must be able to manage his own family well and make his children obey him with all respect. For if a man does not know how to manage his own family, how can he care for the church of God? He must be mature in the faith, so that he does not swell up with pride and be condemned, as the Devil was. He should be a man who is respected by the people outside the church, so that he will not be disgraced and fall into the Devil's trap.
>
> 1 Timothy 3:1–7

The successful leadership of a growing congregation has become a complex responsibility in our era. Any number of tasks will be starting up at a given time; some will be in full stride, and others will be winding down in their life cycle. Change will be occurring constantly, for life itself is ever-changing, and very little remains constant in the art of leadership. Since each of your activities will have to be approached and managed in a somewhat different manner, flexibility is of the essence.

Men and women come to church membership with attitudes, values, expectations, and beliefs that are uniquely their own. Each member may subscribe to some collection of core beliefs, but it is safe to assume that no two people in any congregation see eye to eye on everything. It is more than a cliché to say that when two or more people agree all the time, at least one of them has stopped thinking. This wide diversity of thought makes it necessary for a minister to create an encompassing vision that can appeal to people with their own different ideas of what is important.

Begin by winning the members to a personal commitment to Christ. Then paint a vision of discipleship in a community of God, made up of loving, mutually supportive people. Use broad and bold strokes. Don't become entangled in pet hobbies of your own. As you mature as a pastoral leader you will discover an amazing fact—the things that seem so desperately important in your ministry at twenty-five or thirty years of age are often inconsequential at forty-five or fifty.

No less a preacher than Billy Graham matured in this manner. In his youth he wholeheartedly supported military force and the development and willingness to build earth-killing bombs in a great anti-Communist crusade. Now he reports that he was naive and ignorant of just what he was supporting. And while he once preached against the U.S.S.R. with great zeal, he now preaches in that country. He finally realized that there are more practicing Christians in the Soviet Union than there are Communists.

I find that pastors who compromise their effectiveness in the ministry do so more by focusing on nonessentials and speculating on theological constructs than by any other practice. I am not anti-theology or anti-philosophy, of course, but theories in themselves seldom meet the needs of people who should be receiving gospel preaching and an opportunity to serve God and humankind. Know and reach *all* the congregation. Set the stage so that energetic and successful middle managers, teachers, artists, and other professional people will find satisfaction in worshiping and serving with you. Become their inspiration and role model as they use their abilities for Christ and the church as ever-maturing disciples.

Harold Grey, a close friend of mine who built a grand fellowship of many different coalitions, taught this to his associates. I sat in his office one afternoon when a young couple in the congregation asked Harold to form a couples' association. My friend agreed enthusiastically. He showed the youngsters where to find materials they should read about such a ministry, took some seed money from his pastoral account, told them how to publicize the new group, and then persuaded them to chair the steering committee. They were glowing with anticipation as they left Harold's study. They were ready to get started with something that was important to them personally and could be shared with others. After we were alone, Harold told me: "It's a miracle the things that can be done when you captivate the interests of people and release their creativity. Especially if the pastor doesn't care who gets the credit. I always try to see where the people are going, get a head start on them, and let them persuade me to lead the parish."

I have also seen Harold take a lay-leader aside to whisper that something had slipped, that so-and-so needed help. The member was thus encouraged to step into the committee to give support as necessary and then drop out when the program was running wellagain. Harold spent thirty-six years in that parish. He started with a little white meeting-house on the creek and built it into a powerhouse of faith, hope, and love.

Parish Influences

A successful leadership approach is the by-product of many elements. You simply cannot say to prospective members, "Come to *my* church so *I* can be a successful minister." That is somewhat like asking *me* to work the next twenty-seven Saturday mornings so *you* can have a chalet in Aspen. Something important is lost when translating your motivation to mine. In the last analysis, you can build a significant ministry only by persuading the members to accept your influence and your vision, by making the parish so attractive a community that other men and women will want to become a part of it.

Just yesterday, on a religious talk show, I heard the pastor of a very successful congregation tell the host that the church had grown well because "God had blessed it." That was true enough, and I would not argue with such temporal and spiritual evaluation by this modest man. However, I could not help thinking of the old joke about the pastor and the farmer. As they walked through the fields and past the well-filled barns, the minister kept telling the landowner how much God had blessed him, how God had given him such riches. The farmer finally grunted and quipped. "True enough, Reverend, but you should have seen the place when God had it by himself." Touché!

The pastor on that talk show is a devout, hard-working person and I respect him. He is also as skilled in creating the good by-products that lead to church growth as any minister I know. The parish there wasn't much when the Lord had it in partnership with the previous ministers! Not only has the present pastor learned how to preach outstanding sermons, he has learned how to harness the commitment and cooperation of a larger and larger community of Christian believers. He has multiplied his influence through sound social and cultural activities in which the members find spiritual meaning.

When I was much younger than I am now, I pastored a growing congregation for a denominational superintendent who appeared not to understand how to extend a church's influence into the community. Not only did he oppose much of what we younger ministers were doing, he insisted we minister in precisely his manner. He told me that I was wrong for refusing to preach sermons in which women were taught to wear their hair in the style his mother used at the turn of the century. He criticized the congregation for having a church kitchen and enjoying potluck dinners on special occasions. He preached sermons in which he condemned the "evils" of civil rights for black people, voting rights for all, television sets, computers, and stereo equipment. He also insisted that I not permit any of the congregation's youngsters to play high school and college sports—at a time when the local high-school football team—from tackle to tackle—was made up of youngsters from my congregation!

When I told the superintendent that he had it all wrong— that I encouraged them to play, that I had played football in college myself, and that the boys had voted me chaplain—he became furious. In fact, his anger became uncontrollable. Such people, regardless of their sincerity, are fighting change and are unable to serve any community well. They certainly miss the point of how to influence a congregation toward mature disci-

pleship. There are many social avenues through which successful congregations can move to meet those psychospiritual
needs that bind people together in a cause greater than themselves.

Parish Progression

In a recent study conducted by a local research group in a
large sample of Minnesota congregations, the researchers began with the assumption that the church members would be
concerned about nuclear war, pollution of the environment,
civil-rights violations, and other problems publicized in the media. The researchers were astonished to discover that the
almost-universal congregational concern was the identity of the
local church. Who are we? Why are we here? What should we be
doing now? In other words, many congregations are confused
about the message being taught and the methods being used.
Follow this equation:

$$\text{PARISH PROGRESSION} = f\,(C^4)$$

The four C's are *confusion, communication, commitment,* and
cooperation.

You must move a significant number of members past the
crippling element of *confusion*—through *communication,* to
commitment, and on to *cooperation.*

Confusion. The last thing a confused congregation needs
(and according to the study, many of them were confused in
several key areas) is a minister who is not sure of his or her own
mind. A pastor who approaches leadership from a Pauline-New
Testament perspective can move beyond confusion. This is
where one's theology is crucial. Either get your theology
straight that Christ indeed is Lord or quit mucking around and
muddying up the waters for the faithful of the parish.

I am convinced that congregations without a sense of identity
are that way because they have little depth of commitment to
Christ and his church. I do not deny anyone's redemption, of
course. That is between the person and God. But in all-too-many
cases people see themselves as disciples of Christ only *after* identifying themselves nationally as Americans, Britons, Canadi-

ans, and so on, *after* seeing themselves as employees of a certain company, *after* belonging to a political party, *after* whatever. Church membership is down about sixth or seventh on their list of affiliations. No wonder so many congregations have identity problems! No wonder strong pastoral leadership is needed today.

You must take the initiative in presenting Christ and the church as the key affiliation of your own life and then persuade a growing number of people to see it the same way. To put it simply, the local church and the church universal are much more important to people in growing congregations than they are to people in static parishes. Of course, today's static church will be dying tomorrow.

Communication. How does one convince people of the need for a vital church in the community? Communicate through preaching and persuading, in forum groups and Bible studies, through newsletters. Share the high expectations you hold for the parish. Do what you can to develop positive attitudes and mature beliefs. Teach the members to express the high affirmations that become self-fulfilling prophecies. Remember that writers as far apart as Viktor Frankl and Eric Hoffer teach that most people find it more important to be useful than to be wealthy. Communicate ways to connect this trait to ways of serving God and humankind.

Commitment. Wholehearted dedication is part and parcel of the Christian life, so recommend it continually to your members. Don't let anyone stop with redemption, since being born again is but the entry into the Christian life. Be persistent. In Jesus' day, only three went all the way to the garden with him. And then they fell asleep!

Work in innovative ways to develop a sense of committed discipleship among the members—as I see the churches in Africa, Latin America, the Pacific Islands, and even in Malaysia doing. Their commitment to the church and their neighbors has resulted in remarkable church growth.

Cooperation. This is the logical outcome of the type of communication that leads to commitment, which transcends personal interests. Just as building a great dam, starting a new business, or electing a candidate to office is a cooperative venture, so is the numerical and spiritual growth of a congregation.

When people share the responsibilities and rewards of spiritual growth, they cooperate to bring about the good things they want. I have never taught that it is easy to move a community of believers through the C^4 process, but it can and is being done. In my community, I have only to visit Mount Olivet Lutheran, Park Avenue United Methodist, Colonial Church of Christ, and Grace Baptist to find committed, cooperative people who take the gospel seriously. And they represent but a few of the successful congregations in Minneapolis alone. Each one of them has a strong parish leader who has remained in place long enough to make major changes in the lives of the people.

Congregational Differences

As I study the church today, I find that it cannot be seen from any one perspective. Yet there is a strong temptation to assume that what one sees personally is all there is, or is what the church should become universally. There are theological, governance, and worship differences that reflect cultural realities as much as spiritual attitudes. The differences range from highly structured Roman Catholic practices to the experiential emphasis of charismatic groups. There is a multitude of shadings between, and that is only in the United States!

As I work around the world in my consulting, I can detect a great stirring in the church. No later than the year 2025, the population center of Christianity will have moved well south of the equator. Black African Christianity is gaining almost twelve members for every one it loses. The Latin church in Central and South America has launched out in new directions to serve the poor and distressed rather than to protect and placate the rich and powerful. The Pacific church is boiling with enthusiasm, and Christians there create their own hymns, theology, and worship practices. A young friend of mine from New Guinea, whose father hunted human heads when I first met him, serves as a missionary to Australia—while he teaches microbiology in a Sydney university! The indigenous Methodist Church in the Islamic nation of Malaysia is the fastest-growing branch of Christendom in Southeast Asia.

Unfortunately, a great many people in American congregations and denominations become angry when the greater-world church no longer supports the economic, military, or political goals of the United States. Why should African, Bolivian, or Papuan Christians pull our chestnuts from the economic or military fires of this era? Are we implying that *our* cultural and national customs are the heart of Christianity?

In light of the great differences occurring in Christianity, a successful pastor must work within what would be called the house style in business and industry. For example, not only do Baptist and Presbyterian congregations differ from those of the United Church of Christ, but Baptist, Congregational, and United Methodist parishes differ internally. Some congregations want a smooth-preaching, scholarly minister who challenges them intellectually. For others, a rough-and-tumble approach will be more relevant to the factory workers who make up most of the parish membership. As pastor, you must learn to cope with the distinctive needs and varying backgrounds of your membership, for that is what ministry is all about. There are very few cookie-cutter Christians in the real world.

When I went from New Mexico to my second parish in Louisiana, some of the members were uncomfortable upon learning that I had studied in California. Quite a few of the French fishing locals feared I would prove to be a stuffed shirt who would not appreciate their rural ways. I felt their concern very soon and did my best to reassure them. I preached the very finest sermons I could prepare, called on the families, drank their Cajun coffee, brought in new members, started innovative programs, baptized the converts, married the young people, and buried the dead. They accepted me for my concern, but my final breakthrough with the men came in a more dramatic manner.

When some of the newness wore off, some of the men tentatively invited me to go duck hunting with them. I sensed that they expected me to faint at the sight of a shotgun. I accepted, although I had to borrow a gun since I had none of my own at the time. We went deep into the Grand Marais marsh, which the men knew so well because of their commercial fishing. We settled into a duck blind, and I was informed that as their guest I had first shot.

Impulsively and rather impishly, I began asking a number of naive questions about ducks and hunting, questions about altitude, speed, and so on. Without ever saying so, I convinced them that I knew nothing about hunting water birds. We waited quite a while before a flight of mallards circled and began letting down into range. When I knew that I had them, I brought the gun up and fired three times. The three leading birds folded and fell, and the retrievers splashed into the water to get them.

When I sat down to shove three more shells into the old pump gun, the silence in the blind was awesome. I waited. When no spoke, I murmured, "That doesn't seem too hard. If I had known how easy it is, I would have taken up hunting years ago. I do think this gun pulls a little to the left, however." I was grinning from ear to ear.

The chairman of the church board realized he had had his leg pulled and looked reproachfully at me. "Brudder DeVille," he said sadly, "dis ain't the fust time you shot duck." He was right. In all fairness I had to tell them that I shot the highest gunnery runs ever recorded in the Fifth Air Force before I was twenty years old. They accepted me after that as a man among men.

Next I went to pastor a church in the western suburbs of Cincinnati. The skills that served me well in rural Louisiana were of little use at the Fairmont Church in an affluent urban community. The house style there was completely different, and I had to adapt considerably in order to be anywhere near as successful interpersonally.

Be flexible and adaptable as a parish leader. Accept the fact that the ministry is a high-stress profession and that you must become a problem solver and decision maker in order to serve effectively (doing the right things in the parish) and efficiently (doing those things right). Learn how to cope with anxiety and ambiguity, for other people will disagree with you. Be thankful for challenges, for it is when life is difficult that the church most needs and best rewards bold leadership. Do what Napoleon Bonaparte recommended to his colonels. Battles, he said, are won by officers who plunge into the thick of things to find out what is going on. Get among the people to know what they need. Another lesson from Bonaparte is that there are no bad churches—only bad pastors. Napoleon actually reported there are no bad regiments—only bad colonels—but you understand my point.

When you analyze a thousand people (or even a few hundred) at random from a community, the group will form a bell-shaped curve of distribution (Most people will cluster around a mid-point or "average" in the degree to which they possess the characteristic in question. As either extreme is approached, there is a decreasingly smaller proportion of the population involved.) for virtually all human traits. Although some people assume that great differences exist between different states, regions, and nations, that is not so. Since every group faces the same kinds of human problems in a finite number of ways, it is up to the pastor to understand and influence what occurs by harnessing the best human abilities and skills found in that normal distribution of talent and traits. Styles will be different but, beyond that, people are pretty much the same everywhere.

Parish Participation

After my speech to a group of pastors a few months ago, a young woman in her first pastorate asked how she could get her lay-leaders to mature as decision makers for the congregation. I doubt my answer was what she wanted to hear, but I am convinced it is correct. I told her: "Find what they are interested in about the church, put them to work doing it, and give them the opportunity to fail, without throwing them to the wolves."

I am convinced that the only route to personal maturity in serving Christ and the church is through making responsible choices. Surely you have discovered that you personally learn more from your mistakes than from your successes! When you lose rather than win, you are compelled to go back to find what went wrong rather than basking in everyone's admiring approval. What would your life have become without challenging parents, demanding teachers and professors, and hard-nosed bosses who would not let you compromise on second best? Each person must stretch his or her abilities and talents to become a mature Christian.

Coercing or conditioning people to move in a lock-step approach may make them compliant, but that is never a good way to develop parish participation. Unfortunately, the ministry does attract its share of people who have hidden psychological needs to manipulate people for personal reasons. After all, if one's weaknesses can be miraculously transformed into God's message and will for everyone else, the minister's status is guaranteed, at least in his or her own mind.

FIGURE 4 **Task Organization**

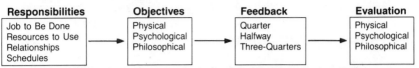

Responsibilities	Objectives	Feedback	Evaluation
Job to Be Done Resources to Use Relationships Schedules	Physical Psychological Philosophical	Quarter Halfway Three-Quarters	Physical Psychological Philosophical

Identify *responsibilities* and *objectives* before beginning work. Through *feedback*, verify that you are on course three times during the program or project, correcting as needed. *Evaluate* success/failure at end.

Achieving parish participation requires identifying and motivating members to complete tasks that promote growth within the congregation. Mature parish participation stems from the physical, psychological, and philosophical aspects of group interaction. There must be something in the activities and work that stirs the heart as well as moves the hands and feet, if the people are to assume the ownership of the church's responsibilities and rewards. Simply accepting busyness produces few disciples for Christ.

As your members become more committed to their tasks, you will find the guidelines in figure 4 especially helpful in keeping them on course. This chart has been valuable to me as I planned activities within the parishes I served or when I was a lay-leader.

Once the specific tasks are chosen, teach the workers to use the chart for their own benefit. Have the people decide which responsibilities they will assume. Remember that you are dealing with a volunteer group who must be influenced and persuaded! After choosing the tasks to complete, they should be persuaded to identify the objectives to be reached. (How can they know if they have been successful if there are no standards toward which to aim?) Parish workers should also plan on identifying quarter point, halfway, and three-quarter point goals as a means of acquiring feedback. When things are not working well, it is much easier to adapt at the quarter point than at the three-quarter mark.

If problems occur, have the responsible people resolve them without your intervention whenever possible. By training them to venture out in faith, by giving them the materials and help they need, and by refusing to devalue people when they make mistakes, you are contributing to their maturity in a participating parish. Remember, more people want to be "useful" than want to become rich. Drawing from that deep human need can assure growth in all its different phases.

Politics or Relationships?

I was at a meeting a few months ago when a young pastor snorted loudly and protested that ability always plays a less-important part in a minister's promotion than church politics. As I listened to his frustration, I felt tempted to welcome him to the real world of interpersonal relationships. His mistake was to forget that there is universal human trait to deal with and help people we already know. Given a choice of promoting either an acquaintance or a stranger, of working with the two, or of recommending them, we typically prefer turning to the one with the known traits. We all try to avoid unpleasant surprises in our relationships.

A successful pastor will thus have to use the so-called political power available to each leader, although I prefer the less-pejorative term *relational power* to describe this very normal human tendency. This is the power base a pastor must develop through interpersonal acceptance by dynamic, achievement-oriented people in a congregational network. Even Paul, when in a Roman prison, called for people he knew to help him in his ministry. *Relational power is the utilization of relationships to reach personally desirable goals that are compatible with the congregation's mission and house style.*

Notice that my definition does not exclude the use of the pastor's authoritative/achievement influence. Instead, relational influence *builds on* the preceding two. This is but another way of saying that the harnessing of the congregation's relationships is an exercise in personal influence. Of course, you must work within the denomination's interpretation of Scripture and theology and follow the house style of your congregation. Even if individual Southern Baptists or United Methodists have been known to serve cocktails on occasion, you can rest assured that as a group they are not going to invest in a roadhouse to finance their youth camps! That is completely out of character, although more than a few churches and denominations hold investments in secular businesses and industries that deal in legitimate products. There *is* a difference!

If you are an ambitious minister who believes that succeeding in God's work is more fulfilling than failing, accept the fact that personal relationships will be part of the successful leadership as long as the church lasts. This aspect of human interaction may be illogical or even irrational at times, but it must be considered when exercising parish leadership. Love, friendship, mutual respect, and trust are crucial in every kind of congregation.

Striking a Balance

Take time to think about the way you interact with the people who can make or break your career. Plan ahead for contingency choices so you can use the appropriate type of leadership when circumstances shift.

In a summer tornado last year, a local church group demonstrated the need for a minister to shift gears from "participation" to "personal power" and back again. The storm blew away the building's roof. When Pastor Robert Hess's wife called him at a Rotary Club planning session, he quickly excused himself to his associates and rushed home. He did not call a meeting to discuss the matter but set in operation the church's "telephone tree" to call out the troops. The network quickly contacted everyone who was physically fit and within reach of a phone. By the time Robert was in his work clothes, the congregation had descended on the disaster en masse. Pastor Hess stood atop the steps and took charge as people arrived, setting them to work with hand trucks, wheelbarrows, plastic sheeting, rope, and whatever else was available. He set up an account with a nearby hardware store to supply what was needed, with never so much as a by-your-leave from the board or the treasurer. With a rainstorm in the offing, there was no other way.

The next day, however, rather than dominating the hastily convened congregational meeting, the young minister called on the expertise of a banker member of the congregation, worked with the finance committee, and put everything to discussion and a vote. He was correct in both cases, of course. When the roof has fallen in, either figuratively or literally, you must take charge in a strong authoritative manner. Put the people to work. They deserve and need no less. Then, when there is time to

Figure 5 **Combining Authoritative/Achievement Influences**

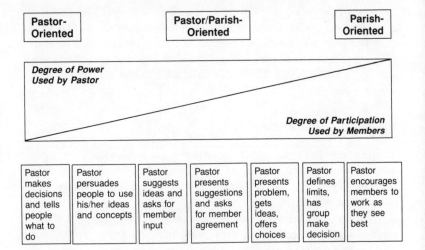

Pastor makes decisions and tells people what to do	Pastor persuades people to use his/her ideas and concepts	Pastor suggests ideas and asks for member input	Pastor presents suggestions and asks for member agreement	Pastor presents problem, gets ideas, offers choices	Pastor defines limits, has group make decision	Pastor encourages members to work as they see best

contemplate and to consider the ramifications of suggestions and proposals, use the appropriate style for that situation. Your ministry will be more successful because of your ability to shift approaches from time to time.

Figure 5 is a diagram that shows how a pastor's use of authoritative/achievement influences can create the kind of participation that makes a church great in its outreach. It has been adapted from "How to Choose a Leadership Pattern" by Robert Tannenbaum and Warren Schmidt in *Management Classics,* edited by J. M. Ivancevich and M. Matteson. Glenview, Ill.: Scott Foresman, 1981.

There is usually a negative correlation between the use of power and authority and the degree of parish participation that develops. Different house styles and situations will play a part, but the greatest degree of commitment and parish participation occurs when members have the freedom to grow and mature through the leading of the Holy Spirit.

3

Involving Your People

In the field of selling products and services—where success occurs only as the salesperson solves problems for customers—I find a consistent principle in operation. It is this: Although no one wants to be abused, taken advantage of, or sold items of no value, all of us like to have nice things for ourselves or for the people we care about.

The same general principle holds true in persuading or influencing people to do the work needed to create a strong congregation. You cannot tell people: "Come to my church, tithe, and work hard, so *I* can have a great career." If you even feel that way about member participation, your nonverbal communication will repulse the kind of perceptive people you need to help a congregation grow.

And yet, such diverse writers as longshoreman-philosopher Eric Hoffer and psychiatrist-psychologist Viktor Frankl agree with Jesus that normal men and women need to be needed. It is more important to psychospiritually healthy people to be useful than to be wealthy or even politically free. Thus, when the gospel is preached and exemplified in love and mutual support within a congregation, a growing number of people will take advantage of the opportunity to contribute in ways that make them feel good about being Christians.

My brothers, what good is it for someone to say that he has faith if his actions do not prove it? Can that faith save him? Suppose there are brothers or sisters who need clothes and don't have enough to

eat. What good is there in your saying to them, "God bless you!
Keep warm and eat well!"—if you don't give them the necessities
of life? So it is with faith: if it is alone and includes no actions,
then it is dead.

James 2:14–17

History is filled with wonderful examples of Christians who
caught a vision of how they could work and contribute to the
family of God. Usually they react in this manner because someone caught their attention and showed them how to harness
their faith in ways that contributed in different situations and
circumstances.

Personal Motivation

One of the basic points of Jesus' gospel is that we are to avoid
being selfish in our relationships with God and with other
people. On the other hand, as I work with men and women from
many denominations and congregations, I find that virtually
everyone is self-centered to some degree. I have never known
anyone who was completely altruistic, and if there were such a
person, the world would soon crucify him. We almost always
personalize everything that happens to us. It was Freud who
quipped that no person with a toothache could be in love. Nor
can we seriously discuss great theological or philosophical issues when both nostrils are plugged tight by a sinus attack. We
are too egocentric to exercise a great deal of grace under pressure unless we have matured spiritually.

As I understand it, making a commitment of one's life to
Christ is suposed to weaken the bonds of selfishness that
prompt us to take advantage of others. On the other hand, a
person living without some degree of self-centeredness would
not be motivated to accomplish a great deal. Psychospiritually
healthy people expect to gain some benefits from their actions
and contributions. We want to feel good about being useful.
That's all right, and I believe that God calls us to succeed in our
work and is disappointed when we fail. Certainly *we* are unhappy when we do not succeed.

With our unique human ability to substitute symbolic rewards for tangible payoffs, we are often most satisfied when our

successes are psychological and spiritual. And that's also all right, since we do not live by bread alone. In fact, since the Reformation, we in the church have had few tangible rewards to offer. The church does, however, work much better within the total human experience than any other kind of organization, especially those working with just tangible rewards as motivators. In a previous book called *Nice Guys Finish First*, I told about four naval chaplains who, while aboard a torpedoed cruiser in a sea battle against a Japanese fleet, gave their life preservers to seamen struggling up from the engine room. Obviously, the way these men felt about themselves had a powerful influence on their lives. In fact, I have to believe they were putting into practice the very principle of James's that I quoted above. When the *Dorchester* sank, all four chaplains died because they had acted on their spiritual beliefs. I have never heard of four Christians with any higher motivation from their faith.

Entire books have been written about the motives that people bring to their worship, work, love, and play. Yet, when we clear away all the symbolism and emotional baggage with which we approach life, we discover the basic fact that motivation is never something one person does to another. *Motivation is an internal, personal movement toward some goal, which can be described in the fact that people alone or in groups consistently do what is important to themselves.*

We are all born motivated, live motivated, and will probably die motivated to do the things that we find important to us or to the people who are important to us. *I* will never be committed to working the next twenty-seven Saturday mornings so *you* can have a chalet in Colorado. I *have* offered to help my son and his children plant fruit trees behind their home, although I will probably not live long enough to see them come to maturity. On the other hand, if you will let me use your chalet when I'm on one of my trips to the mountains, I may be willing to negotiate my Saturday mornings for a while.

The Motivational Pyramid

My own theory of motivation lends itself to a model that looks like Abraham Maslow's, although it is quite different. I will explain as it becomes appropriate.

FIGURE 6 **Motivational Pyramid**

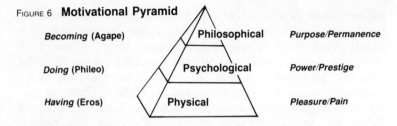

Becoming (Agape)   Philosophical   *Purpose/Permanence*

Doing (Phileo)   Psychological   *Power/Prestige*

Having (Eros)   Physical   *Pleasure/Pain*

This pyramid can be thought of as an extension of the human personality into the interrelated worlds of worship, work, love, and play that each person inhabits. I believe that the model in figure 6 is physically, psychologically, and philosophically sound. It follows the progression of psychological discoveries from 1880 to 1980. It also makes use of the biological discoveries about the brain from the medulla up through the cortex.

Physical Motivation. When a person is motivated only in the physical aspects of life, the needs for food, water, shelter, sex, and clothing are predominant. Each of these needs must be consistently satisfied before a person can devote much time or thought to conditions higher in the pyramid. (Remember Sigmund Freud's quip about a person with a toothache being unable to think seriously about being in love?) In his book *Baa Baa Black Sheep,* Greg Boyington wrote at length about wartime prisoners held without enough food, clothing, or medical care. As they lived on a near-starvation diet, they lost interest in loved ones, sex, winning the war, and everything except surviving. The prisoners fantasized by the hour about food—about gathering, preparing, and eating food. They would steal supplies from the guards and, despite being beaten, would go back to steal once more. It was only as they returned to the United States and were fed and cared for adequately that they moved past the physical level of motivation. Normally, most people are past that first tier, where "having" is all-important.

Human motivation begins with the pleasure/pain principle. Normal men and women seek pleasure and avoid pain. We all intuitively know that Freud was correct in postulating this view of life. For example, we know that it is better to keep one's hand out of a car door. As behaviorist B. F. Skinner wrote, food, shelter, transportation, and entertainment are reinforcers, sources of pleasure through which we meet our "having" needs. In an affluent society, where most people have their basic physical needs consistently met, the typical pastor finds little motivational power at this level of the pyramid.

Psychological Motivation. The second level of the pyramid continues with the power/prestige principle formulated by Alfred Adler when he broke with Freud. Adler had decided that mere seeking of pleasure and avoiding of pain was too simple an explanation for overall human motivation. Adler was right, of course, as we can learn by observing wealthy people still hard at work although they have all the money they require to meet life's physical needs. We all want prestige and self-esteem in order to feel good about ourselves, so the "doing" needs become most important at this level. This represents the fact that we all need to be useful in some way. Yet, men and women are more complex than that, as we shall see next.

Philosophical Motivation. In the third aspect of motivation, the typical person must move on to the purpose/permanence principle, alluded to by Viktor Frankl in the approach to psychospiritual health he calls Logotherapy and I more fully described and formulated in my previous books. In this last tier of motivation, each person reaches for fulfillment of his or her potential—working to mature in all that makes life the best it can be. "Becoming" is now the predominant motivation.

Motivation in the Church of Today

In an affluent society such as ours, the church may not be as involved in meeting physical needs as in Africa or Latin America. Yet, we do have serious pockets of poverty and must be responsive to that. I have mentioned Colonial Church, which donates fifty thousand dollars a year to African relief, and Park Avenue United Methodist, which hires fifty young people each summer to work in a number of crucial areas in its inner-city community. Both work from a deep evangelical faith that manifests itself in broad social concerns, and both congregations have become communities of faith *and* works.

Follow the motivational progression, for it is psychospiritually healthy. Drawing on what you have learned about the motivational pyramid, create opportunities for boys and girls and men and women to participate at every level in accord with

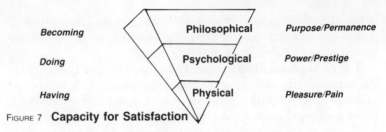

Becoming   **Philosophical**   *Purpose/Permanence*

Doing   **Psychological**   *Power/Prestige*

Having   **Physical**   *Pleasure/Pain*

FIGURE 7 **Capacity for Satisfaction**

their age and interests. If their "having" needs are met, give the kids things to do according to their stage of maturity—games of all kinds, camping trips and outings, projects to complete in the church and the community. For the young people in adolescence, tie the activities to their school projects, courtship rituals, and career interests.

In Abraham Maslow's concept of motivation and life, he made the mistake of assuming that once a person reached a higher tier (he postulated five rather than three) he or she could not regress. I disagree, since you *can* regress and suffer from it. A person who seeks satisfaction at the "doing" level but is frustrated may well turn back with a vengeance to the "having" level and eat or sleep far too much. Another man or woman who fails to reach the philosophical level that comes with increasing maturity, or who regresses because of a specific failure, may spend his or her life in a ceaseless round of "doing" activities that become self-defeating because they are satiating. When, through circumstances or choice, a person is denied satisfaction all through the pyramid of motivation, he or she remains restless and unsatisfied. Take your congregation, individually and collectively, to a higher plane than simple church busyness. Help them find a perma- nent sense of purpose through spiritual growth.

To understand how satiation can defeat a person who does not mature in the concepts that motivate him or her, turn the pyra- mid over. It then looks like figure 7.

In the physical aspects of life, the capacity for satisfaction is limited. How many steaks can you eat before you are nauseated by the thought of more food? Not very many. How many Mer- cedes automobiles can you own before the urge to buy another is pointless? Very few. The same self-limiting factor exists in the psychological aspects of life. The capacity for satisfaction is greater there, but it is hardly limitless. I have known a great many people who become burned out by their work—by the things they are "doing" to meet their psychological and "having" needs.

It is in the upper tier, where life is open-ended because it is spiritual, that we can go on and on to become what God makes possible to us. It is in the spiritual realm that we can go on to infinity and, if our faith is correct, to eternity also. Therefore, as a Christian leader who works with people in a complex society, remember that this progression exists, that it is a normal one, and that the activities you develop for your congregation should fit within this framework. (I will write about specifics in other sections of this book.) Utilize the innate human motivation to "have," to "do" and to "become" by leading your group so people consistently win *pleasure* rather than pain at the physical level, *prestige* and *esteem* rather than humiliation at the psychological level, and *purpose and permanence* rather than meaninglessness at the spiritual or philosophical level. When you utilize this view of how and why people do the things they do and become what they can be, incredible things can be accomplished, especially with high expectations and positive attitudes.

Attitudes—Good and Bad

Each person I have known well in my personal relationships, or in my counseling or consulting, reached adulthood with unique characteristics and traits. Every human being combines inherited traits, childhood experiences, and crucial choices so different from everyone else's that we cannot find two fingerprints alike, to say nothing of two minds and sets of emotions. Nevertheless, our human attitudes and expectations can be boiled down to four categories, as Thomas Harris did in his book *I'M OK, YOU'RE OK*.

It seems to me, as I work with pastors in different settings, that a great many of them fail to realize this. Each parishioner has almost total control of the expectations that determine whether or not he or she will be effective and successful. I find in talking to them that few pastors recognize that their members are all working from a game plan that either focuses on individual strengths or fails to use them well.

In most people's lives, the stage is set for healthy living (or a lack of it) by the dominant psychological attitudes each child accepts for himself by combining inherited traits, environmental experiences, and key choices. There are four crucial attitudes affecting every person's expectations about life and his or her place in the scheme of things. They are:

1. **The Superiority Attitude**—"I'm all right, but you are not all right."
2. **The Inferiority Attitude**—"I'm not all right, but you are all right."
3. **The Hopeless Attitude**—"Neither you nor I are all right."
4. **The Accepting Attitude**—"Both of us are all right."

The Superiority Attitude. When you try to work with someone with a superiority attitude, the first impulse may be to call that attitude a superiority "complex," especially if the person is successful in carrying off his charade of exaggerated self-worth. Actually, this is a psychological overcompensation in which the user is protecting himself from consistently feeling bad about himself. Anyone who has to pretend to himself and to others that he alone—and possibly those who agree with him constantly—is the only one with an ability to make decisions for a congregation is obviously a troubled person. Yet every pastor has to deal with determined, eccentric people who know that they alone have the wisdom to make sound religious decisions. In his excellent little book of a generation ago, *Neurotics in the Church*, Robert St. Clair told of people who have a "special revelation" from God, who feel that their insights make it necessary for everyone else to submit to them. They put inordinate pressure on pastors, of course.

When I was pastoring in Louisiana in my youth, I grieved for a poor, beleaguered friend of mine who was trying to minister to a congregation that had two such men in it. Their struggle for personal power was self-justified as a new message from God to the congregation and became so fundamental to all the church activities that they could not even resolve what color to paint the sanctuary. Neither self-appointed prophet would yield, so the board painted half of the church beige and the other half lime green! Although the church became a laughingstock in the community, the two men with the superiority attitudes felt they had won some kind of victory. Naturally, the congregation never did accomplish anything for God.

The Inferiority Attitude. At one time I heard a successful pastor make the statement that you cannot build a church with a certain type of people. I resented his evaluation of human effectiveness at the time but have since come to believe that he was correct. You cannot build with people who hold fast to an inferiority attitude. People who say, "*you* are all right, *you* are competent enough to get the work of God done, but *I* am not— because I have no talent, no strength, no calling or no money," are the bane of every pastor who believes my point that God calls us to succeed rather than fail.

As I am writing this book, my wife, Roberta DeVille, is the lay-leader/chair of our official church board. In other denominations she would be called the congregational president, the head deacon, or the senior warden. We have a succession in which the lay-leader first becomes an associate and then progresses to senior lay-leader status. In the middle year of our succession, the associate lay-leader is responsible for managing the finance campaign for the following year. When that occurred for Roberta, she put the move on me to recruit about fifty men to make home calls with pledge cards.

When I did that for her, spending several evenings a week for several weeks, I found once again that it was those already busy with careers, families, and social activities who were most willing to help with the calling. A great many of the people who had the time to help made excuses that emphasized their own inferiority attitudes. They made excuses: "I'm too shy to talk to people about money," or "I've never made a fool of myself in this manner, and I'm not about to start now," or "My wife would never agree to my going with your group," or "I went in 1962 and got a door slammed in my face." Thus spoke the inferiority-oriented men, upon whom a congregation can seldom be built.

The Hopeless Attitude. People with a hopeless attitude, who say that *nothing* can be done (so why try?) are doubly cursed. In childhood, such people likely rejected their own worth and that of others as well. A great many become inept, frustrated people like assassins Lee Harvey Oswald and Sirhan Sirhan, hopeless losers who finally lash out at people they detest because they are succeeding in life though apparently without merit. A few, like Albert Camus and Jean-Paul Sartre, attacked a "hopeless" society with books rather than with weapons.

It has always been one message of the church that Christ receives hopeless and inferior men and women. Redemption is for the down-and-out as well as for the up-and-in. Every minister worth his or her salt can tell of awesome acts of grace through which converted people became marvelous bearers of the Christian vision. Nevertheless, most of the people who carry the load in a congregation are the ones who do good work in other settings as well, partly because they recognize that few situations are hopeless.

The Accepting Attitude. The final attitude emphasizes acceptance and states honestly and freely that we are redeemed peers—together in a fellowship of faith and works and without any need for pretense. My own congregation deliberately works at holding this attitude collectively despite the failures of some to grow spiritually. Several years ago I brought some guests to a banquet in our fellowship hall. Twelve men were serving us, and as the evening progressed it dawned on me that six of the men were very wealthy and the others were employed at such work as carpentry, manufacturing, or sales. I turned to my outside guests and explained the situation. Then I asked them to try to pick out the wealthy men. They could not do so, of course.

An accepting attitude is more than simply a good feeling about other people. It is virtually a spiritual philosophy of life. It is a healthy Christian position that enables a person who lives in Christ to relate effectively and well with a wide variety of men and women. It is a powerful belief in the redemptive grace of God and a willingness to seek and hold positive human relationships. If you have an accepting attitude, you will give to others the respect, support, and cooperation they deserve when working together. There is then no need for you to win every discussion, campaign, and plan to prove that you are better than everyone else—especially not to prove it to yourself—since everyone else has long since seen through our shams in close, interpersonal relationships.

Some time ago I was lecturing a congregation's adult forum when a woman became quite distressed as I spoke of the need for

Christians to hold accepting attitudes that imply "I'm all right—and you're all right." She said, "We're *all* wretched sinners who deserve God's wrath, and there's nothing worth accepting in ourselves." I have run into that hopeless attitude before and heard it called Christianity, which it is not. It is a way of confusing the theological *humility* we finite and imperfect humans often feel in the presence of a holy God with the psychological *humiliation* that springs from a distorted and unhappy childhood. The first attitude is based on the awe that comes from the contemplation of God and his creation and from being the recipient of his redeeming grace. The other springs from a long-unhealed childhood wound as devastating as a cancer. Christians have every reason to reject the negative attitudes about themselves and others while working through positive attitudes about living as God's people.

The Power of High Expectations

Researchers are just now beginning to understand the dramatic power that faith, trust, imagination, and high expectations hold over each person's life. It makes no difference that people with self-defeating attitudes and resultant low expectations blame their unhappy condition on fate, poor circumstances, or the shortcomings of others. We now know that each person has an individual game plan that is consistently followed. Such a life plan directs us toward activities and relationships that are beneficial or harmful or sometimes a combination of both.

I know a young woman, now in her mid-thirties, who had somehow created for herself a soap-opera scenario for life. At the age of eighteen, in rebellion against her parents' religious faith, she moved in with a manipulative, alcoholic man, had a child by him, and let him dominate her life for six or more years. He spent every dollar she earned at her jobs as a waitress. When she broke up with him, she moved in with another man, also older, who likewise let her earn enough to pay the rent, make payments on a large automobile, and pay for his alcohol and dope.

When she broke up with him, she came to me for counseling, complaining bitterly that men were nothing but rip-off artists. Then, in the midst of our sessions, she met another man, another hard drinker who held jobs only when he chose and expected her to pay the rent and support his habit. She immediately moved in with him and took over his responsibilities, as she had done with the others.

She explained that in each case she had loved the man so much that she "couldn't let him go." It is apparent that she has a game plan for her life that includes the belief that she must be "in love" at all times, that men who have problems need her more than others, and that she somehow cannot relate to men who are making their way well in life. Her expectations are such that she has spent a decade and a half with users and abusers of women. I wonder if she will ever learn that a far better way of life can be hers if she changes her defeating expectations to positive ones. Her game plan for life is self-fulfilling. So it is with most people in a congregation as well as with the collective game plan that the church membership is following. We can maintain a set of positive expectations that defies stagnation, financial shortfalls, and declining membership—or we can program defeatism into the life of the congregation.

If you have inherited or unknowingly brought in people with low expectations and negative attitudes, you will have trouble getting such men or women to accept a greater vision. A great man of faith I know, a true pietist of our age, inherited a declining inner-city church many years ago. The neighborhood was changing as blacks and Mexicans moved in and members of the congregation left in droves for the suburbs. Churches all around were closing their doors or becoming closed fortresses to which people came only for services and then left without making any impact on the community.

Peter Warren told me when I interviewed him, "I didn't come to Madison Bluff Church to preside over a dying congregation." And he proved it! He evaluated the situation, scoured the community, and hired a capable and enthusiastic associate. In time, slowly at first, the church there became one of the finest inner-city, multiracial congregations in the nation. Peter paid the price in blood, tears, toil, and sweat—to paraphrase Winston Churchill—but he was successful in a thousand ways for a multitude of lives.

At lunch a few months ago, I asked Peter what the turning point was. When did he feel that they were going to make it all come out right? He shook his head and sighed: "When we got rid of the haters." He went on to explain that he had a group of men and women who had made up their minds to keep the church as it had been when they were young couples there. Others hated the black children and the other ethnic groups Peter and his growing band of workers brought in. Still others opposed every attempt to buy busses and establish summer camps for the children, fought to block the organization of a nursery for working mothers, tried to fire the strong associate who came from Chicago with a plan for working with rather than against the neighborhood. The dissidents almost succeeded, until Peter stood in the board meeting and stated: " Some of you have the mistaken idea that we are here today to consider the ministry of Dean Hawkins. We are not! We are here today to consider the parallel ministries of Dean Hawkins *and* Peter Warren. What you decide about one, you decide about the other."

This giant of a pastor had to let go those who would destroy the church rather than adapt to a new vision of what God's work at Madison Bluff could become. He laboriously created a new set of expectations to replace those no longer adequate for the community. He succeeded because positive attitudes and high expectations have the power of life or death over our plans, our contributions, and over our very existence.

A Winning Game Plan

For centuries we have seen that men and women who were doing responsible tasks with a positive attitude had a better chance of surviving than those who were drifting or negative in outlook. Pastors, physicians, and nurses have been known to work through epidemics that were killing thousands of people without ever contracting the disease, and this occurred in the days before effective vaccines. Perceptive people often wondered why such people survived. I decided to find out for myself after a late-evening conversation about such things with Viktor Frankl.

When I was psychology chairman at Westminster College, I selected ten psychology majors and minors, all alert, healthy young men and women who were good hypnotic subjects, as I had discovered in previous tests. I put the ten in deep hypnotic trances (no, hypnosis is not a tool of Satan but simply a function of the autonomic nervous system). I left them with the post-hypnotic suggestion that life was good, that they were happy and working at tasks that were important to themselves and to society. I awakened them and, in the middle of the week, re-inforced the suggestion for each student. At the end of the week I had blood samples drawn from each person. A week later we repeated the procedure with the same students. This time I left them with the post-hypnotic suggestion that they were un-happy, doing badly in their studies, and not likely to ever do anything of value to society. I reinforced these negative feelings midway in the week and took samples of blood at week's end.

The results were astonishing. For each student, without ex-ception, the agglutination titer against bacilli infection was many times higher when the students felt a deep satisfaction with life. Therefore, when the physicians, nurses, and pastors were doing their jobs as they felt they should in past epidemics, they were more resistant to disease, discouragement, even death. Likewise, the values, attitudes, and expectations held by the members of a congregation often mean the difference be-tween life or death. They virtually always mean the difference between winning and losing in everyday activities.

Men and women who understand the power of expectations usually organize and develop sound congregations. This week I received a brochure from the Oral Roberts Evangelistic Associa-tion. It was called *Abundant Life,* and in the publication was an article about something called Faith-Talk. As I read the prayer and an accompanying article, it became apparent to me that Roberts was teaching the use of high expectations in the lives of his followers. Is this not what Jesus meant when he said that with faith we shall move mountains?

Each congregation can be said to have a positive or a negative electrode implanted in its psychospiritual center of gravity. A negative electrode draws failure and disappointment like an old-fashioned lightning rod attracts electricity during a storm. Negativism induces unhappiness, conflicts, and failure because these results are compatible with the congregation's lack of vi-sion.

On the other hand, a positive set of expectations, which a pastor can develop through example, teaching, and preaching, (if he remains in place long enough to change lives with God's help) attracts good planning, thoughtful decisions, supportive relationships, and committed-cooperative work. The satisfactions that result from this kind of winning game plan are no more the result of luck than the disappointments in a losing one. Success in winning the consistent commitment of your people comes from your own high expectations for them, sound planning, successful persuasion, and hard work. The crucial aspect is your realization that you can learn to shape attitudes and expectations within yourself and for other people, rather than being maneuvered and manipulated by what comes through circumstances.

4

Personality Patterns
That Shape Relationships

It should be obvious to any perceptive person that God has not used a cookie cutter to stamp out people in a well-organized manufacturing process. The work of creation is much too complex to be fully comprehended within the parameters of the human mind. A wise New England grandmother who was reflecting on her years of experience with people of all kinds, supposedly told her listeners that men and women of all kinds, colors, and inclinations "are mostly all alike—but the differences they have are powerfully important." So it is at all times in a minister's work.

There are different kinds of spiritual gifts, but the same Spirit gives them. There are different ways of serving, but the same Lord is served. There are different abilities to perform service, but the same God gives ability to all for their particular service. The Spirit's presence is shown in some way in each person for the good of all. The Spirit gives one person a message full of wisdom, while to another person the same Spirit gives a message full of knowledge. One and the same Spirit gives faith to one person, while to another person he gives the power to heal. The Spirit gives one person the power to work miracles; to another, the gift of speaking God's message; and to yet another, the ability to tell the difference between gifts that come from the Spirit and those that do not. To one person he gives the ability to speak in strange tongues, and to another he gives the ability to explain what is

said. But it is one and the same Spirit who does all this; as he
wishes, he gives a different gift to each person.

1 Corinthians 12:4–11

There are no two people in the world, pastors or parishioners,
who are identical in the way they think and react. Even identical twins have had different experiences that shape them in
unique ways despite their hereditary sameness. Nevertheless,
from as long ago as the Golden Age of ancient Greece, scholars
and ordinary men and women have searched for recurring patterns in attitudes and actions among people. As we deal with
others in our worship, work, love, and play, we seem to look
automatically and unconsciously for consistent trends in the
people around us. There are two major reasons for this.

First of all, if we can find a way to identify what is important to someone else, we can make life easier for ourselves by
predicting his or her behavior in advance. Almost every person I
have talked to about the importance of personality patterns in
relationships admits to having created a system for identifying
the way other people are going to behave. Unfortunately, many
such schemes are fragmented, biased, and otherwise so flawed
as to be virtually useless. Most personal systems come from
childhood, when we were reacting to a handful of people who
might or might not have been representing anyone but themselves. As adults we typically think in terms of Democrats differing from Republicans, men from women, professional clergy
from volunteer members, French from Germans, labor from
management, blacks from white or red, and in other categories
that are too broad and much too simplistic to be of value in one's
ministry or any other frame of reference.

In the second place, as we mature and choose our own system
of predicting behavior as a means of protecting ourselves and
enhancing our lives, we do so because we have learned that
people *do* behave in consistent patterns. I do, you do, and so does
every other person on God's good earth! Our attitudes and actions seem to be burned within our very neural pathways from
infancy onward.

Personality Differentiation

As far as I know, Socrates was the first to leave a written
record about the various temperaments he found by observing

the people of his day. Carl G. Jung, the great Swiss psychologist, went further with his view of psyche types. Pastor Tim LaHaye has done some work in the area, as have psychologists David Merrill, John Gier, and many others. My book *Nice Guys Finish First* popularized the concept of personality patterns internationally. The book was accompanied by my Personality Pattern Assessment, which is now used under the name The Self-Profile. The Personal Dynamics Institute of Minneapolis has marketed some hundred thousand or more of the instruments, so I am well pleased with their reliability and validity.

We now know that personality patterns do exist, that understanding them can neutralize many unnecessary conflicts, that harnessing them can enhance the success of any congregation, and that building on one's patterned strengths and eliminating one's weaknesses can empower a pastoral career. Best of all, the utilization of valid research into patterns takes the use of a system far beyond the luck-of-the-draw that goes into most catch-as-catch-can systems people normally use.

You have undoubtedly seen the differences I am speaking about. At a staff or board meeting, Elaine will be teetering on the edge of her chair, impatient with details that are being discussed long after she has decided what she is going to do. Andrew will still be talking about options yet to be discussed so he can remain comfortable in reaching group consensus. Matt will be concerned how the congregation will *feel* about the choices being made and so on. And, if you meet with the same men and women five years later, you will probably find the same kinds of concerns guiding their attitudes and actions. Unfortunately, without an understanding of patterns, it is too easy for people to become impatient with one another, to attribute to others insincere motives or anti-spiritual biases. After all, we are all egocentric, and anyone who frustrates *me* must be wrong!

Our personality patterns are normally developed early in childhood from a number of factors. Most traditional psychologists attribute personality to a combination of heredity and environment. I cannot leave it that simply, however, because of my view of free will. It appears to me, from my biases and from my research, that personality-pattern development is more complex. There is an element of choice continually involved. For, if the human mind has *any* capacity at all, it is the ability to consider a great many options in a very short while.

Each person, as he or she matures, combines inherited traits, environmental experiences, *and* personal choices as a means of being as comfortable as possible in life. That very complex process can be shown in an equation that looks like this:

PERSONALITY PATTERN = f (Heredity × Environment × Choices)

Because each child at the moment of conception has more genetic traits to draw from than there are grains of sand on all the beaches of the earth, no two people ever start with exactly the same raw material. (Even identical twins, who start with the same hereditary makeup, will have experienced different physiological stimuli in the womb, which will have already influenced their personality at birth.) Those differences are then multiplied by environmental experiences, and that product multiplies once more by the personal choices one makes about life and his or her place in the world. Therefore, one child may reach school age with a pattern that looks like

$$P/P = f (H^{18} \times E^{22} \times C^{15}),$$
while another looks like
$$P/P = f (H^{10} \times E^{27} \times C^{35}).$$

Great differences exist between the two patterns.

Keep in mind that once the pattern has jelled early in life, there is little anyone can do about changing it. It takes years or a great traumatic experience to shift a basic personality pattern. Furthermore, there is usually no need to change patterns, for all my research reveals that one's personality is not nearly so important in building a successful life as the way one uses it, in the ministry or any other sphere.

When I began researching this book for pastors, I interviewed twenty senior ministers of dynamic, growing congregations in various cities around the United States. Because I have been researching and writing about leadership and interpersonal relationships for a long time, I was not surprised to find that no two of the successful pastors were alike in their personality patterns.

John Hansen is a big, blond Scandinavian giant. He is bold, somewhat gruff in his relationships, and runs a tight ship for staff and members alike. No one ever wonders who is in control of that congregation. John is the captain, and as he makes the key decisions he often reminds me of the actor John Wayne.

Equally successful is Harold Langhorne, of another parish just a few miles from John's. Harold is quiet-spoken, mild in his relationships, always supportive, and excellent at working *through* his staff and members. He seldom forces an issue the way John does, and he reminds me a great deal of the actor Glenn Ford. I could, of course, go on and point out different personality patterns among the ministers I interviewed, but that would be getting ahead of myself.

I should say one thing, however. Despite having different patterns, the twenty pastors have created loving, supportive Christian communities of their parishes. And I am convinced that no congregation will reach its true potential to love and serve God and humankind until the parish leaders accept differing patterns and styles as normal and necessary and harness the varied strengths of their membership. People are given different gifts, and it is foolish to try to cram everyone into the same mold. We must understand our great, God-given diversity and use it wisely and well.

Behavioral Response Patterns

I have discovered in my research that men and women interact along two key behavioral lines. One trend can be considered a horizontal response to life, while the other can be thought of as vertical.

When we are threatened, frustrated, or simply confused, we normally follow what many psychologists call the fight-or-flight syndrome. We attack or we flee—we become aggressive or we become apathetic about using our survival skills. In a "civilized" world, when we need to protect our egos, we may internalize this fight-or-flight reaction. The human race has learned two crucial things. A lion couldn't eat you and your family if you had already killed it; and it couldn't eat you if it couldn't catch you. These traits seem to be part and parcel of the human baggage, although they are usually moderated and unspoken in our era.

74

Figure 8 **Cooperation-and-Competition Continuum**

There is another aspect of the human condition that is instrumental in developing personality patterns. This is the conceal-or-reveal syndrome. As we are growing up, most of us learn that it is sometimes best to show our feelings and motives to other people and sometimes wise to hide them. My grandchildren are quite adept at this already, even the two-year-old! They climb into my lap with hugs and kisses, revealing their emotions for both sincere and ulterior reasons. I have no doubt that they love me as I love them, but they are also very good at wheedling dimes and quarters from me. Just as *I* did with Grandpa a long time ago!

But, when things go wrong and conflict develops, the little dears have also learned to conceal their resentment. They have learned at an early age to use the conceal-or-reveal syndrome in their relationships. And that is perfectly acceptable in a civilized organization in which the emotions and interests of many different people must be coordinated. Tact, civility, politeness, and mutual respect are essential in human interactions.

As a pastor, you cannot succeed by hitting on the head every member who opposes your plans for the future. Nor can you build a strong congregation by running screaming from every challenge. You must balance between a poker-faced refusal to reveal your feelings and babbling everything you feel and think.

In civilized settings, where people symbolize and negotiate their choices, the fight-or-flight syndrome becomes a cooperation-and-competition continuum. My research shows that some people are most comfortable when cooperating in their interpersonal relationships. They cooperate regarding the direction of conversation, the use of money, people, and time. Other men and women, with just as deep concern and spirituality, react competitively to control conversation, activities, and relationships. The continuum from highly cooperative to greatly competitive looks like figure 8.

We have assumed for the sake of convenience that there are six categories of behavior on the cooperation-competition scale

FIGURE 9 **Conceal-or-Reveal Continuum**

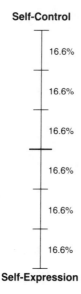

and ranked a random sample of people accordingly. We then find that about 16.6 percent of the sample would fall in each section. At the extreme ends of the continuum would be placed people with strong tendencies toward either cooperation or competition. People who are highly cooperative seem generally thoughtful of those around them. They appear able to negotiate settlement of disagreements smoothly and unwilling to make abrupt decisions that overlook the viewpoints of all concerned. On the other hand, men and women who are at the competitive end of the scale come across as verbal, willing and able to make fast choices, and dominant in their relationships and activities.

Everything said in the previous two paragraphs refers to relationships between people. It has little to do with the normal human desire to be useful, to win status, or to successfully finish a life task. I shall return to those aspects later.

Using a similar approach, the conceal-or-reveal continuum in civilized activities and organizations could be represented by figure 9.

There is a continuum from poker-faced self-control at the top extreme to uncontrolled self-expression at the bottom. In nei-

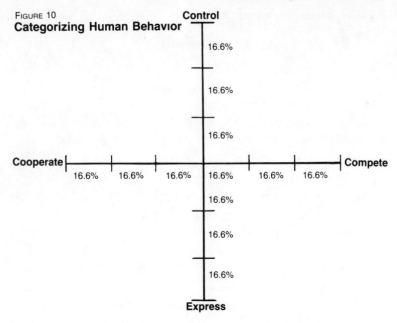

FIGURE 10
Categorizing Human Behavior

ther distribution is there a best place to be. However, you would not want to be at the extreme end of either continuum, since inflexible behavior and attitudes make it hard for other people to accept you and difficult for you to accept those who are different.

When the two continuums are combined, they can be represented by the diagram in figure 10. The end points of the axis represent four categories of behavior: Control, Compete, Express, Cooperate.

Extrapolating further, we arrive at figure 11, which was developed from the data secured with my Self-Profile instrument. The men and women, (there are no significant differences within the genders) who are in the outer circle have the indicated traits to a greater degree. Those in the middle circle have them somewhat less, and those in the center have the traits to the least degree. You can see that the four sets of traits form four primary personality patterns. These styles represent Controlling, Entertaining, Supporting, and Comprehending patterns. They are shown in relationship to each other on the chart.

People with *Controlling* personality patterns have a consis-

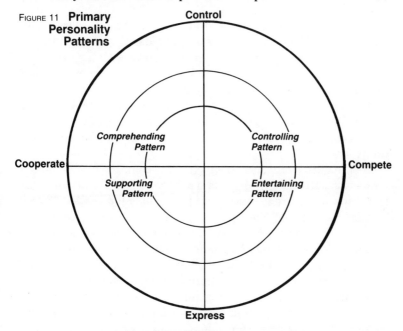

FIGURE 11 **Primary Personality Patterns**

Control

Cooperate

Compete

Comprehending Pattern

Controlling Pattern

Supporting Pattern

Entertaining Pattern

Express

tent tendency to use self-control and to compete in their interpersonal relationships. They tend to be dominant individuals such as Billy Graham, Bella Abzug, Richard Nixon, and Jeane Kirkpatrick, our former United Nations ambassador. These are men and women who do not joke a great deal and who are not especially concerned with the emotions of others. They are task-oriented "command specialists" who remain comfortable interpersonally by *telling others what to do*. By using their traits well, Controllers can become very successful ministerial leaders.

People with *Entertaining* patterns have a tendency to use both competitiveness and self-expression in their relationships. They are often enthusiastic and can be considered the "emotive specialists" of life and work. Johnny Carson is a man with such a pattern. The singer Beverly Sills, called Bubbles by her friends, is this type of person. So is comedienne Joan Rivers, and so was President Lyndon Johnson. Pastors and others with this pattern can generate a great deal of enthusiasm by *telling others what they feel*.

The *Supporting* pattern is that used by men and women who

openly express their feelings while cooperating interpersonally with others. They generally seem to be deeply involved in the feelings of other people and can be considered the "concern specialists" of life. They often *ask others what they are feeling* as a means of remaining in their personal comfort zone. Ed McMahon of the "Tonight Show," Dinah Shore, Glenn Ford, and President Ronald Reagan share this personality pattern, as do many pastors who use their people-oriented skills to lead their congregations.

People with *Comprehending* patterns combine a tendency to cooperate with others with the use of self-control in their relationships. They are factual in outlook and can be called "information specialists." They are committed to identifying crucial facts before reaching decisions. Such men and women remain in their comfort zones by *asking others what they are doing*. Jimmy Stewart, Eric Sevareid, Katharine Hepburn, and President Jimmy Carter illustrate a Comprehending personality pattern, either in their type-cast acting roles or observable behavior.

My research reveals that people with any of the four primary patterns can be effective and efficient ministers—if they work to maximize their strengths and minimize their weaknesses. They must also accept and utilize people who are different from themselves rather than falling into the "liking trap," which is the temptation to reward and utilize only those people who allow one to remain in his or her own comfort zone.

Pattern Strengths and Weaknesses

After I began evaluating the research, it did not take long to discover that pattern strengths and weaknesses are closely related. In other words, the strengths *become* the weaknesses when pressed too far. A minister with a Supporting pattern may come to grief by accepting too much dialogue from concerned people when the time has come to make a firm decision and get on with important tasks. An Entertainer, with his or her tendency to joke and tell stories, may come across as a clown when other people want to settle down and seriously discuss a major problem. Comprehenders who want facts will have to stop asking for more information at some point and project the work of the church on faith.

Few people, however, show how strengths become weaknesses more clearly than Walter DeLacourt, who pastors a congregation in Ohio. Walter had been very effective in a small congregation, which he took to considerable success through his dynamic, Controlling style. He worked sixteen hours a day, made most of the decisions and generally told everyone what they must do. He really told them! Because he was the pastor when new members arrived, most people accepted his personality pattern. I suppose that anyone who did not like his style did not join. The time came, however, when this successful minister, an outer-edge Controller, faltered badly. He was called to a large sophisticated congregation in Toledo but went in without understanding that the parish had its own way of doing things, that there was a strong core of lay-leaders from business, industry, and the professions with their own styles and interests.

Walter came in like a storm, tried to impose his own vision on the congregation without first winning them to himself, and almost ruined the sense of fellowship that existed there. Personally powerful people rebelled. Walter could get nothing he wanted through the board and within two years was gone. His strengths had become his weaknesses when used inappropriately and pressed too far.

Comprehenders serve a parish best when they investigate and analyze information, searching for and discovering the needs of the congregation but not making that an end in itself. A pastor must often make choices from incomplete information. If a comprehender waits for all information to come in before making a difficult decision, it will be made by default, or needed action may be stalemated.

Controllers serve a parish best when they implement and direct the work of the congregation. Their action-oriented pattern makes it easier to get things done. As with Walter, however, the typical weakness is to take risks that could be minimized by research and by ignoring the emotions and needs of the members.

Entertainers serve a parish best when they inspire and reinforce spiritual, positive activities. Every church needs exciting, stimulating leadership to be at its best. The pastor with this pattern may be popular but sometimes gets into trouble by assuming that having conceived of and designed a program means that it is working well. Entertaining pastors usually need to discipline themselves to do the routine, detail work of the parish and actively seek feedback from the congregation.

Supporters serve a parish best when they educate and counsel their people to excellence. They are especially effective when negotiation and compromise are indicated. They may get into trouble by continuing to tolerate diverse opinions and discussion when the time has come to develop a plan and work together on it.

Any minister who insists on seeing only one pattern as normal or effective—usually because he or she is outer-edge in that pattern—damages a congregation. First of all, such a pastor may actually be working with or ministering to only one-fourth of the congregation's potential. In the second place, no one has the insight to choose only those men and women who will allow one to remain in his or her own comfort zone. Misunderstandings and conflicts can follow that have nothing to do with spirituality, orthodoxy, commitment, or devotion.

Pattern-Based Conflicts

Most of the pattern-originated conflicts I see occur diagonally across the distribution. When two people do not share one of the four traits—cooperation, competition, self-control, or self-expression—they often have trouble relating well with each other. For example, Comprehenders and Supporters share cooperative traits, so there is a basis for understanding and mutual trust. Since Supporters and Controllers, like Entertainers and Comprehenders, share none of the four key traits, understanding is more difficult. This makes it more likely that such people will also misunderstand each other's motives and expectations, especially if one or the other is near the extreme end on a trait continuum.

I know of a parish where the conflict between a task-oriented senior pastor and his people-oriented associate caused great harm to the younger person's career and to the congregation's well-being. Henry Anderson was a Controller who had taken charge of a small city congregation and built it into a powerful community of faith in a thirty-year period. There were influential men and women on the governing board, but they had all come in on Henry's terms over many years. Besides, Henry's bark was much worse than his bite, and he worked long and hard for God and the church of the Lord Jesus Christ. He did, however, think of the younger ministers as his assistants rather than as associates. It was not easy for the young seminarians to cope with Henry.

Trouble broke out when Howard Pitkin arrived. The young man, with a Supporting pattern of behavior, had served as an infantry officer in Vietnam and had his own ideas of what was important in a congregation. Before long, the fat was in the fire! The young man explained:

> He's a beast! He wants to interfere in everything I do. If I take a group of kids out camping, he calls to make sure I'm there. He insists on selecting the programs I use and what my sermon topics are to be. He cares nothing about the way others feel and orders people around like animals. I can't stand the bully.

The senior pastor saw things differently. His view was:

> Howard is a marshmallow! He never tells the kids what to do but is always letting them cry to him. They twist him around their little fingers rather than going on to do what they know they should. The man's a wimp!

Actually, I found Howard to be one of the best counseling ministers I have ever known, while Henry was not nearly so good in dealing with human pain. The conflict broadened, the congregation began to take sides, and the young man had to leave. That, however, did not end the problem. Because Henry was determined to dominate the situation, the next associate chosen was a fearful, easily manipulated person who failed to last out the year. Henry was simply too close to the edge, too determined that only Controllers like himself made good pastors, to work well with his associates.

Controllers and Supporters or Entertainers and Comprehenders most often have conflicts resulting from pattern differences. It is when the behavior styles lie diagonally across the circle that most tension and stress is created in interpersonal relationships. There is more possibility for a positive interaction

F<small>IGURE</small> 12   **Effects of Tension and Stress on Performance**

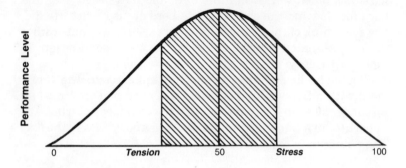

when the individuals involved have different personality patterns, yet share a common trait as shown in figure 11—such as Supporters and Entertainers, who share expressive tendencies.

Patterns and Stress

Each person's comfort zone is that span of attitudes, values, and expectations from which he gets the most done for the least amount of effort. Many things can cause tension, obviously, but tension in itself is not necessarily bad. Tension can be the result of having to do something important in a limited amount of time, and few people would accomplish anything were it not for the tensions of life. On the other hand, when tension mounts and crosses over to become stress, productivity falls rapidly. Tension in relationships is normal, but stress is debilitating. The comparison looks like figure 12.

When a person's or a congregation's tension increases to the peak (the shaded portion), performance increases appropriately. If pressures continue beyond that point, however, the performance level begins to decline. When the stress becomes all a person or an organization can bear, a collapse occurs and nothing good is done—virtually all performance stops.

Predicting Behavior

At the beginning of this chapter, I wrote that we all use systems to predict how people will interact with us, in order to avoid

FIGURE 13 **Predicting Behavior Shifts**

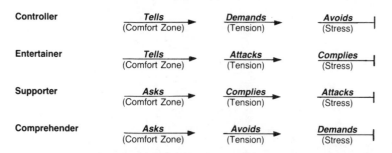

being abused or misused and to influence others. I stated that most such systems were too simple and generalized to be useful. Figure 13 diagrams a prediction method that can be very valuable to you. The shifts in behavior are according to the fight-or-flight and the conceal-or-reveal syndromes. They are more or less predictable for each of the four basic personality types discussed above.

Controllers, for example, remain in their comfort zones by telling people what to do. If that doesn't work, tension increases and they become autocratic and demand that others do as they want. If that fails, in times of stress, they avoid situations and people they cannot control. The process is indicated for each of the patterns.

The ability to predict behavioral shifts is very valuable to a minister in the leadership of a congregation. By learning to anticipate, you can judge how much pressure to put on an amiable Supporter before he or she explodes in frustration or attacks in anger. You can even deliberately frustrate an outer-limits Controller so that he or she will avoid you and you can get on with your work! On the other hand, when you find a Comprehender taking a firm stand and demanding certain activities or relationships, it is time to reduce the pressure.

It is even more important to understand what your own pattern is, as a means of managing your own tension and stress. I have no factual data but suspect that most pastors want to see themselves as Supporters—nice guys and gals who live with human-centered care and compassion in their relationships. That is all to the good, although being a Supporter does not make a minister any better in the total work than any of the

FIGURE 14 **Personality Pattern Organizer**

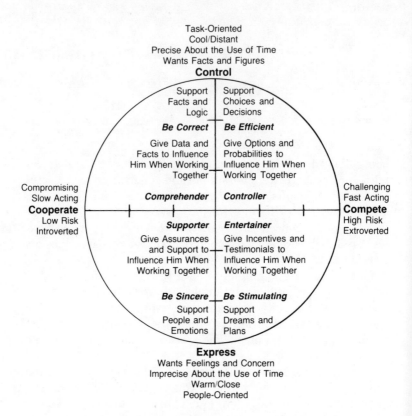

other patterns. Keep in mind that Dwight D. Eisenhower had a Supporting pattern. He put together the greatest military coalition of history—some fourteen languages were spoken by his soldiers. Yet historians repeatedly speak of the general's temper, which could flare when least expected. Eisenhower was going through the progression shown for Supporters. Not only was he tense, he was under severe stress much of the time. And why not? He was putting a quarter-million men on the beach at Normandy and, for all he knew, they would be killed by sunset! No wonder he lashed out at others according to his pattern. By learning the trends, you can predict interpersonal behavior rather than reacting after the fact.

Finally, the Personality Pattern Organizer in figure 14 is useful in identifying the patterns of others and in most effectively influencing them. The descriptions on the outside of the circle tell you how to identify a person's pattern, while the suggestions on the inside tell you what to do to influence a person with that pattern.

PART 2

Situational Leadership

5

Logical Parish Leadership— Problem Solving

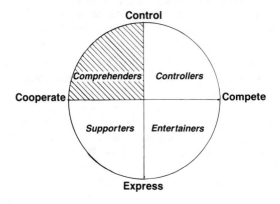

Control

Comprehenders | *Controllers*

Cooperate | **Compete**

Supporters | *Entertainers*

Express

In this and the next three chapters, we will apply what has been learned about the four basic personality patterns to the handling of specific facets of your overall parish responsibilities. "Situational leadership" implies that what you have discovered about your own customary style of interaction with others can help you determine how best to approach your challenges and apply your skills in an effective manner. Since your very strengths can become weaknesses when allowed free rein, a selective tempering with the strong points of other personality patterns is usually a wise course of action, especially in touchy situations. The threefold goal, of course, is to activate an ongoing church outreach, inspire a healthy spirit of fellowship within your membership, and maximize your personal success as a congregational leader.

The people who fit in the upper-left quadrant of the Personality Pattern distribution chart are the ones I call *Comprehenders* in my Self-Profile. They combine cooperative and control traits in such a way that they remind you of President Jimmy Carter and the acting roles of Jimmy Stewart or Katharine Hepburn. If you need to, refer to the preceding chapter to get a better understanding of the Comprehending pattern. Such men and women come across to others as cool in their relationships, reluctant to take interpersonal risks, and precise about the use of resources and time. They can be considered the concept-oriented, information experts of life.

Of course, Comprehenders, as previously stated, feel all the normal emotions that more outgoing people do, but they tend to use more self-control in expressing them. However, church leaders should never focus so intently on meeting their own needs or returning to their personal comfort zones that they neglect the needs of their followers.

> We who are strong in the faith ought to help the weak to carry their burdens. We should not please ourselves. Instead, we should all please our brothers for their own good, in order to build them up in the faith. For Christ did not please himself. Instead, as the scripture says, "The insults which are hurled at you have fallen on me. . . ." And may God, the source of *patience* and *encouragement,* enable you to have the same point of view among yourselves by following the example of Christ Jesus, so that all of you together may praise with one voice the God and Father of our Lord Jesus Christ [italics added].
>
> Romans 15:1–3, 5–6

Comprehenders use a number of interpersonal methods to collect the information that allows them to remain in their comfort zones. They do several things that can be grouped under the phrase *asking others what they are doing.*

These traits combine according to the $P = f(H \times E \times C)$ equation that appeared earlier in the book. Because they are information experts, Comprehenders tend to use organized and logical methods that seem natural to them. They remain most comfortable and effective when gathering enough facts to use in making the best possible decisions. Such men and women are typically at their best as leaders when they can poke and pry to learn the maximum about people, procedures, and processes. They are most efficient when making logical, factual decisions and are very uncomfortable when forced to work from inadequate knowledge. As a rule, Comprehenders do not like to make great quantum leaps. Like Jacob, when his sons were returning from Egypt, they want to see the loaded wagons before burning any bridges. Every congregation, when it draws from a normal distribution of men and women in any community, will have about twenty-five percent of its people in this category. About one-fourth of all pastors also operate from this personality pattern.

If you will pause for a moment here, it will become obvious to you that anyone who approaches pastoral leadership and interpersonal relationships with such a well-organized and logical method can be extremely valuable to the success of any congregation or parish. Few churches will ever succeed without the kind of planning and problem solving that Jesus spoke about in the parable of the man who was caught short in building a high tower.

Borrowing the Comprehender's Strengths

The most obvious strength that a Comprehending pastor brings to the work of God in the local parish is the ability to utilize resources and relationships in an analytic manner. Every pastor needs the ability to look beyond shallow surface manifestations and thereby lower the risks caused by accepting unproven assumptions. The time spent in getting correct information and in allowing superheated emotions to cool down is seldom wasted. In fact, there is a maxim in business management that is appropriate in pastoral leadership when considering the pressure caused by a lack of time. *There is never enough time to do the job right the first time, but there is always time enough to do it right the second time.*

A sound plan based on a good investment of time will enable you to analyze situations, resources, and relationships as a Comprehender does naturally. It will help you improve your

leadership style. If you fit in the right side of the chart as a
Controller or Entertainer, preferring to tell other people what to
do rather than asking what *they* are doing, you may find it
difficult to lead others as a Comprehender does. Controlling and
Entertaining pastors automatically prefer giving orders, instruction, and advice as a means of remaining personally comfortable. But, unless they are wiser than most, they are doing it
for their own benefit and assuming that it is best for the congregation when that is not necessarily so.

According to Patti Roberts in her book *Ashes to Gold,* her
father-in-law, Oral Roberts, approaches his ministry with what
I call a Controlling pattern. After spending all of his adult life
doing things that virtually everyone told him he could not do, he
tells and tells and tells people what is best for them, perhaps not
realizing that the first solution to a problem is seldom the best
answer. When a leader without analytic traits dominates an
organization as completely as Roberts does his, it is almost im-
possible for a more thoughtful person in a subordinate position
to communicate what *should* be considered.

A friend of mine with an Entertaining pattern learned a few
months ago how important it is to listen as well as tell, to use a
Comprehender's skills in his work. On a day that Will Patterson
had set aside to attend a seminar, he stopped by his office to
prepare the liturgy for the Sunday worship service before going
on to his meeting. He hurried through his writing and rushed
out to his car. No sooner had he reached it, however, than a
young, part-time office worker approached him. She had a note
from the church secretary.

In his friendly, lighthearted manner, Will began teasing the
young woman about her coming marriage. It was nothing cruel
but simply a friendly chaffing of someone he liked who was
coming to a major change in her life. She blushed and entered
into the banter with him, so Will slipped the note into his pocket
and thought he would read it on the freeway after he maneuvered his way through traffic. No sooner had he entered the
approach ramp than an accident occurred, and he was almost
fighting for his life in the confusion. By the time he got through,
he had forgotten the note and went to the morning seminar. It
was noon before he recalled the note, read it, and found that he
had blundered.

A prominent member, who had contested several of Will's programs for the church, had been hospitalized and was being prepared for an appendectomy. He wanted to have Will pray with him before the surgery. Will did not get there, of course, and an opportunity to build a better relationship with a rather cool parishioner was lost. It was no great tragedy, but Will lost a bit of ground because he was telling rather than listening.

An Entertainer's or Controller's automatic tendency to give orders must be tempered in order to borrow a Comprehender's strengths. Take time to think logically, to work relationships and situations through mentally in order to make the best possible decision about them. Don't make the mistake of taking charge of every situation and recommending a course of action when you have neither the skill nor the knowledge to know it is the right one. To set out boldly on your pet project without the support and information you need to carry it through to fruition is foolish. It sets the stage for a failure that could be avoided with the skills used by a Comprehender.

This is true not only of programs but in all other aspects of a successful ministry. One situation I learned about seemed simple in retrospect but confused many people and needlessly cost the congregation involved many thousands of dollars. During the eleven o'clock worship service at St. James Church, fumes could be smelled within the sanctuary and in the office. An assistant, the custodian, and several trustees hurriedly checked for fire, saw nothing suspicious and continued with worship. Different people sniffed around all week, smelled nothing, and decided it was an aberration that could be ignored. The following week, as the second worship service began, fumes again could be smelled in the sanctuary and in the church office. Since another inspection revealed nothing dangerous, the following day at a trustee meeting it was decided to bring in a furnace expert. In due time he arrived, went carefully over everything connected with the heating plant, and gave it a clean bill of health. All was well until the following Sunday when fumes could again be detected during the second service.

It was not until several weeks later, when one of the trustees arrived late for worship because of car trouble, that the culprit was found. The youthful driver of one of the church busses, as he waited for his load of youngsters to come out following the first service and Sunday-school, had pulled off to one side of the parking lot. Being thoughtful, he had sat with his engine idling to keep the bus warm in the Minnesota winter—right next to the air intake for the air-conditioning system. It was sucking up the exhaust fumes from the bus and distributing them nicely through the church building!

Then the pastor, obviously not a Comprehender, made a typical blunder. He persuaded the trustees to install a new filtration system rather than simply asking the driver to park somewhere else. It was a case of overkill. After some thousands of dollars were spent, the filters proved to be too restrictive for the old furnace to "breathe" properly. It burned too hot, cracked because of the excess heat, and forced the church to replace the entire system. This was a classic case of fixing something that was not broken, and the plan backfired because the problem was poorly analyzed.

If you are on the right side of the chart, especially if you fall close to the outer border, you may feel that the need to carefully identify all aspects of a problem is cumbersome and a waste of time. It is not! No other process can narrow a complex assortment of raw data down to useful information. Not only is a trial-and-error method too costly in time and money, it is often disastrous. There was nothing funny about the fumes in that church building, a situation allowed to occur off and on because no one seemed interested in how to analyze facts. When you use facts to visualize problems logically, you will have a technique with which to eliminate guesswork and mistakes. Adapt the approach of a Comprehender, even if that is not your "natural" pattern.

The Theory of Problem Analysis

You must realize by now that the consistent analysis of parish problems is a crucial element of sound leadership. After all, nothing is static within the church or in the society each congregation serves. Regardless of how well you and your lay-leaders plan for the future, unplanned events keep occurring and will always force you to solve problems as a means of handling change.

It is counterproductive, even given the way that we of the

church defines "productivity," to work without a logical approach to discover the causes of our problems. As I conducted the research for this book, a number of the pastors I interviewed seemed to feel that I was going to lay another burden on them. Several of them told me they simply lacked the time needed to use a problem-solving tool. They could just "look around" and tell what needed to be done (as with the furnace at St. James Church, I assume!). My answer to them was that no pastor has the time to neglect logical and systematic methods of working in the parish.

If you do not take naturally to the methods used by Comprehenders, and you are perceptive enough to see the need for logical problem solving, develop a systematic cause-and-effect process. Always remember that all problems have causes or they would not occur. Sunday-school attendance does not decline *because* Sunday schools decline. Financial contributions do not slack off *because* contributions fail. Sunday schools decline in attendance because the children in the community have grown up, because another congregation is taking them, because you have terrible teachers and an outdated program. You will not know what has gone wrong or how to correct it unless you investigate the problem logically. The same is true of a decline in contributions or a failure to attract new families and put them to work in something worth doing from *their* point of view.

You can begin by using the same kind of approach that any good researcher uses, whether a scientist, marketing specialist, or political advisor. You must collect information, analyze the data, and eliminate unimportant facts in order to reach the goals you seek. To succeed within the church as a problem-solving pastor, begin with the following systematic process:

Develop factual information about the problems you face. Since it is difficult to manage what you cannot measure, you will have to gather and analyze the facts of a given event or relationship to reach a logical model or picture of the situation. When I teach my management seminars, I recommend that the participants actually plot their information on a flip chart or blackboard. (I prefer a chart because the leaves are turned over and saved for future reference.) Remember that most complex problems are solved in stages. Seldom is the first solution the best, but some of the initial concepts are usually valuable enough to be included in the developing answer.

In addition to keeping ideas and concepts visible for ease of understanding, a flip chart makes it more difficult for yourself and other people to engage in self-deception. As a psychologist, I know very well the human capacity to twist facts and feelings to fit preconceived notions. By plotting out ideas, it is much harder for people to repress and ignore unpleasant but crucial data when solving problems.

When I first conducted meetings in a leadership role, people from different disciplines and with varying responsibilities offered their pet ideas and followed their personal agendas. I often felt overwhelmed with irrelevant and mutually exclusive solutions. There were times when I felt like a Ping-Pong ball being batted back and forth. Therefore I soon began using a visual chart to give the group and myself a frame of reference that could not be ignored.

Spell out precisely the nature of the problem to be solved before seeking the cause. You solve nothing by merely saying that the traffic outside the church building on Sunday morning has become so heavy that the noise detracts from worship. Your statement may be a fact, of course, but it does not analyze the specifics well enough to discover a solution.

You must discover *why* the traffic has increased. Has a new shopping mall opened in your end of town, and will Sunday shopping be a new a fact of life for the next twenty-five years? Did the highway department call for a detour because of six or eight weeks of summer road repair, after which the situation will return to normal? Or is it an indication that a great many new families have moved into the neighborhood, with children who will need a call from your church-schoolteachers? Is the extra traffic a combination of several new factors? You will not be able to solve the problem or profit from the solution until you learn just what the cause is.

You must take time to use a logical approach despite the pressures of the moment. Don't waste your time speculating about ideas and relationships that have nothing to do with the actual problem you are trying to resolve. Use your flip chart. Divide a page in fourths, write WHAT at the top of each quarter of the sheet, and answer these questions:

1. *What* is the *precise nature* of the problem?
2. *What* is the *location* of the problem?
3. *What* is the *frequency* of the problem?
4. *What* is the *result* of the problem?

By answering the Four What's, you can maintain a sharp distinction between *causation* and *correlation*. As you learn to use this approach to identifying problems, the answers will not only reveal what you already know about solving a problem. They will also suggest what you still must learn and point out the need for separating relevant facts from irrelevant ones.

The Problem-Analysis Process

If you have been leading a congregation for any length of time, you and your membership will have developed a number of systems to get the work done. For example, processes and methods will have been developed and people persuaded to get the worshipers seated without confusion and irreverence. Other systems will take care of maintaining the building and grounds, collecting and counting and distributing church funds, recruiting and teaching children in the church school, and all the rest that a successful congregation accomplishes. When the people and the equipment are working well, the outcome seems almost automatic. It is when something goes awry in our utilization of resources and relationships that the unexpected occurs and we realize that a problem must be solved.

In science, education, or business, any departure has long been considered a deviation from a base line of performance. I recall few people besides myself thinking in terms of a deviation from productive relationships as a major problem for the church, but that is what has happened within so many main-line denominations today. Many pastors and denominational officials have marched off into the fog, while many of their people veered back to a less-complicated, more-personalized faith. As such leaders look around, they find fewer and fewer men and women following them—obviously a serious departure of some kind.

Because a typical congregation agrees completely on virtually nothing besides a few tenets of faith and worship and work for God with changing attitudes, values, expectations, be-

Figure 15 **Problem-Analysis Process**

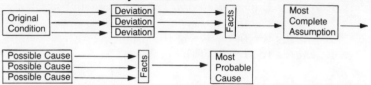

liefs, and choices, every pastor has to be a skilled negotiator and interpersonal leader. Most important, however, he or she will have to be a person who understands the difference between leadership and administration and can differentiate between the use of influence and domination.

When an activity does not reach its expected level of effectiveness and efficiency, a deviation has occurred and must be corrected. For example, let us assume that you want to maintain a base line of 80 percent for church members who are tithers for a one-year duration. Perhaps you have reached this standard in other congregations and have maintained it in your present setting, although your records indicate a slippage in revenue.

You have learned that an increasing number of families and individuals are no longer tithing. You know that a problem exists, but you know little about the precise cause or what should be done about it. You will not know until you become a good researcher by using the Four What's exercise with the people of your congregation who can give you the answers. Figure 15 represents the best process I have ever seen for sifting through the chaff to find the wheat of a well-analyzed problem, the first step in solving it.

To use the problem-analysis process, assume that your revenues begin to slip from the desired tithing base line of 80 percent for all members of more than one year longevity. Start the process by entering the "original condition," or optimum base line in the first box (see figure 16).

By going through church records yourself (or assigning the task to a lay committee), you identify and list on the flip chart the "deviations" that have occurred. You discover that young families with children are the lowest tithers by percentage. Just

Figure 16 **Original Condition**

80%

Figure 17 **Deviations**

64 percent of them have tithed, although that is an increase of 4 percent from the previous year. The retired couples and individuals are at 72 percent, a regression from last year's 75 percent, but you expected that drop because of the effect of inflation on that group's fixed-income levels. That leaves the middle group, those of about 35 to 65 years of age. In the past they carried the load, as 91 percent of them were tithers. Now, by studying the data, you find that this group has slipped enough in participation to draw their figure down to 76 percent. Enter the figures for each group on the chart, including as an analytical aid a plus or minus notation to indicate the change from previously (figure 17).

You realize that while the research indicates that *all three groups* have departed from the base line, the young-family deviation is no real problem, since there was an increased percentage of tithing from the previous year. The facts of the situation are that although the older family units have also decreased their tithing, the middle group has shown the greatest slippage from their former level. You plot the information still further by identifying the middle group as the "cause" in the "most complete assumption" box. In figure 18, the "facts" are statistical and easily summarized into a general assumption about the problem.

There will be times when the "facts" are not so easily discovered. But your search must be methodical in order to make your complete assumption and discover possible causes. In this scenario, you have found the groups with the statistical shortfall and identified the one with the greatest drop, but you have not discovered the reasons. Think through and discuss with the finance committee what the potential causes might be. Go back

Figure 18 **Facts and Most Complete Assumption**

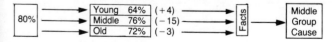

FIGURE 19 **Possible Causes**

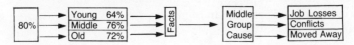

to church records and community data to look for patterns. Is the decline in tithing because of a steel-mill closing on the edge of the city, causing some young families to be out of work and others such as grocery and hardware merchants to fail in business? Has the congregation experienced a conflict that has polarized some of the middle families and caused them to withhold support as a means of protest? Has there been a trend in which some of the twenty- or thirty-dollar-a-week tithing retirees have moved and been replaced by five- or ten-dollar-a-week nontithers? Plot your possible causes as in figure 19.

Going through the church membership records reveals some new facts you have not yet considered. Because the steel mill closed, several managerial families have been transferred to another city. The slippage did not occur all at once but took place over several months, even as you were bringing in new families to keep the average attendance and membership increasing. You talk to several family groups, ask about their commitment to the work of the church, and discover some more facts, all of which you add to your data sheets and analysis chart.

It is now evident that the revenue shortage as tithing families move away for various reasons (taking with them their twenty- or thirty-dollar-a-week pledges) is not being replaced by the smaller, non-tithing gifts of the newer families joining the church. You meet with your finance and membership committees in a joint session with your Council of Ministries (or whatever your denomination calls it) and discuss the findings. Plot it all out on a flip chart so you look like a genius! It should look like figure 20 in the final stage.

FIGURE 20 **Complete Problem-Analysis Chart**

To best use your information about the cause of your problem, you will have to initiate a plan to involve the new families more deeply in the financial demands of the congregation. You will have to preach and teach about tithing as a responsibility of the first magnitude, use church bulletins and letters to communicate this message, and also make certain that new families understand the congregation's expectations before membership is offered.

By walking virtually any church problem through this problem-analysis process, you can discover the most likely cause. It is not a foolproof method, because you or others may bring in the wrong information, but it is far superior to sitting around a table with a dozen people and having each one give you his or her hunches without any confirming data. Although brainstorming has its place, you should always take time to look at the process with a skeptical eye. Challenge your own assumptions by asking other people to find any facts or exceptions that will compromise your answer. It is hard for some people to subject their pet ideas to criticism, but it is far better to find loopholes in advance rather than to discover a mistake after much time and effort has been invested incorrectly. As in the case of the St. James Church furnace, it was an expensive mistake to fix something that was neither broken nor the root cause of the problem!

Potential Problem Analysis

In a previous chapter I told about Controller Henry Anderson, who had such a conflict with his associate minister, Supporter Howard Pitkin, that he made a second mistake in choosing a replacement when Howard left for another parish. Henry brought in a fearful, easily manipulated person who would not challenge him in any way. Unfortunately the new associate failed to win the respect of the youth groups, the official board, and a significant proportion of the church membership. Out of his pain, Henry had crippled his own effectiveness for a year and a half and placed the church in a weakened position. He could have discovered the potential problems he was causing himself and the congregation through a simple potential-problem-analysis process. It can and should be used by you before making any crucial choice in your life or work.

The successful ministers I interviewed for this book all stated that they had to solve effectively many problems that might arise in their parishes. Their consensus was that the parish is a battleground in which people will be maimed emotionally and spiritually unless led wisely to maturity. Even more valuable to the development of a person's ministry or to the growth of a congregation, however, is the ability to keep minor problems from becoming major and harmful. It certainly is easier to nudge a ship back on course by turning the wheel ten degrees than by having to reset the sails and beat against a gale!

I have found in my research and consulting that a great many people in church-leadership positions—pastors, lay members, district superintendents, presiding elders, bishops, and denominational presidents—are all reluctant to admit the possibility of having made a planning mistake. This can be no more than a Controller's or an Entertainer's determination to tell others what to do rather than to listen. Nevertheless, some disasters could have been avoided had someone in authority admitted to himself or herself the possibility of being mistaken. Perhaps that is asking too much of human nature—even redeemed nature.

In his book *Up the Organization,* Robert Townsend insists that the most valuable person in an organization is the jester who keeps the leader from taking himself too seriously. He mentioned a very earthy fellow (from Milwaukee, I believe it was), who cast Townsend's blunders in such graphic pictures that no one wanted to force them through to a disastrous conclusion. There were times when the executive wanted to strangle his assistant, but he had long since learned better than to shut him up.

If you can abandon your ego for a moment and recognize your fallibility as a parish leader, regularly ask yourself the following two questions when planning a new project, as many Comprehenders would do naturally:

What can go wrong in this activity?

What will happen should this plan fail?

If you can also get answers to these two simple questions from your members, lay-leaders, and/or peers, you can regularly avoid the vast majority of needless blunders in your ministry. I have learned that in their emphasis on faith, some ministers feel such questions indicate a lack of dedication. Not so! I cannot help wondering what would have happened if some clear-headed people with the understanding to use a Comprehender's strength had asked cult-figure Jim Jones what he would do should his plan for a South American paradise fail. Perhaps hundreds of lives would have been saved and the church spared a terrible blot.

In St. Louis some years ago, a congregation found a piece of property that looked good for its expansion plans. The price was right—in fact, very reasonable—so an impatient Controlling minister pressed the church to buy it and start building a fine new facility. It was two years before the group discovered that there were reasons why the property was so well priced. Although situated on the flood plain of a small river that flowed harmlessly into the Mississippi most of the time, every two or three years it overflowed its banks, building up to such a flood that it inundated the community for miles downstream.

Potential problem analysis should be conducted in a logical manner. I always use a chart like this to jog my mind into asking and answering the best questions:

What can fail—

When new concepts are presented to the congregation?

When we are running out of time to act?

When complex activities must be coordinated?

When volunteer workers must be relied on?

How will I recognize a potential problem—

Through the knowledge I now have?

Through knowledge I must yet obtain?

How will I deal with potential problems—

That are incidental to my goals?

FIGURE 21 **Outlining Potential Problems**

Potential Problem		
Failure of New Secretary to Perform Well		
	Decisions	
Probable Cause	*Anticipatory*	*Corrective*
1. Can't do the job	Verify references	Train to work better
	Verify grades	Transfer to a job she or he
	Give a trial period	can do well
2. Can't relate to staff	Investigate background	Train interpersonally
3. Doesn't remain long	Verify work record	Increase pay
	Use bonus system	

That are important to my goals?

That are crucial to my goals?

What are the probabilities—

That a serious problem will arise in this?

That a crucial problem will arise in this?

What can I do to eliminate—

The potential causes of my serious problems?

The potential causes of my critical problems?

I often use a simple chart to help me visualize the problems that could arise in different activities. A chart for hiring a secretary would look like figure 21.

When you use this logical method to discover potential problems and identify likely causes of difficulties in advance, you will have to use your personal experience, the congregation's expectations, books such as this, and recommendations from people who are experts to guide your decisions.

Not long ago an architect friend of mine told of a pastor with a Entertaining approach who insisted on designing a new church building without an expert's advice. He knew what he wanted and would allow no one to confuse him with facts. He did not use a potential-problem-analysis process, needless to say, for he had never heard of such a thing.

As he worked on the design, he placed the rest rooms on the

other side of the wall that was immediately behind the baptistry. He may have saved a few thousand dollars in plumbing costs, but the congregation soon voted to tear out the rest rooms and move them. Anytime anyone flushed a toilet, the whooshing roar vibrated through the sanctuary. It gurgled and burped and echoed through the baptistry as the tanks refilled for five minutes or more. It was a design disaster that could have been averted had the pastor asked an expert *what could go wrong* with his design. In the case of building a new church building, the chart would be several pages long. It may take considerable time and effort to develop such a chart for some projects, but it is the height of folly to plunge ahead without asking yourself, your supporters, and your opponents what could go wrong along the way.

When you adapt your approach and utilize the gathering-and-analyzing methods that come naturally to a Comprehender, you can better search and discover the resources and relationships that are necessary to maintain a life-cycle leadership style that transcends your own patterned abilities. Even if you lack the special skills of a Comprehender, you can manage facts logically to solve problems before and after they occur.

6

Objective Parish Leadership —Decision Making

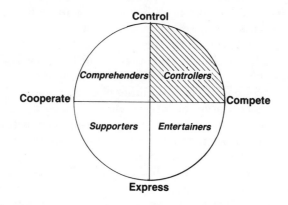

The people who fit in the upper-right quadrant of the Personality Pattern distribution chart are the ones I call Controllers in the Self-Profile. They combine controlling and competitive traits in such a way that they remind you of actor John Wayne, British Prime Minister Margaret Thatcher, and President Richard Nixon. If you are still somewhat unclear about patterns, refer to chapter four to refresh your memory of how they establish their relationships. Men and women with Controlling patterns come across to others as task-oriented, take-charge people who are willing to take interpersonal risks. They are well organized in their activities and can be considered the action experts of life who boldly stand up to say what they feel is important.

> Then Peter *stood up* and with the other eleven disciples and in a *loud voice* began to speak to the crowd. "Fellow Jews and all of you who live in Jerusalem, listen to me and let me *tell* you what this means. These people are not drunk, as you suppose; it is only nine o'clock in the morning. . . ." Peter made his appeal to them and with many other words he *urged* them . . . [italics added].
>
> Acts 2:14–15, 40

I certainly see Peter as a Controller who would fit with many pastors in the upper-right sector of the chart. As I said about the Comprehenders to the left of this position, Controllers tend to suppress their emotions rather than revealing them to just anyone. These self-controlled, task-conscious men and women have a tendency to remain in their comfort zones by giving instructions and issuing orders for other people to follow. They are most at ease when they *tell other people what to do.*

As in the case of the three other primary personality patterns, a Controller's style of interaction developed according to the $P = f(H \times E \times C)$ equation. Following their action orientation, just as Peter did to take the initiative on the day of the Holy Spirit, Controllers automatically and instinctively direct other men and women to do what they believe best. They assume they are at their efficiency peak when they have the interpersonal power to work through any confusion to get things done with a minimum of discussion and feedback. Controllers are typically uneasy with people who want to get too close emotionally, and they avoid a great deal of chitchat. Since they tend not to be introspective, they may not come across as a good leader to people on the left of the chart—the Comprehenders or Supporters who want and need discussion before committing themselves or others to a course of action.

Controllers who are toward the outer edge of the circle may come across as Peter often did, giving the impression of being impatient and unwilling to draw from others the degree of cooperation they would give with a little persuasion. About one-fourth of all pastors have this pattern, and so does that proportion of the members in a typical congregation. Of course, in smaller groups the numbers are more likely to be skewed than in a large church.

If you will think about it for a moment, it will be quite obvious that a pastor who approaches congregational leadership in such a dynamic and challenging fashion can be very successful in directing his church in God's work. Few churches will prosper without the kind of implementing-and-directing skills used automatically and naturally by Controllers. Every parish needs a decision-maker, and this ability can be cultivated by even those pastors who do not have the Controlling pattern in their natural makeup.

Borrowing the Controller's Strengths

The most useful human trait that a Controlling parish leader brings to the work of God is the ability to direct the utilization of resources and relationships in a forthright and bold manner. Although one requires other skills to succeed, any effective leader must often be brave enough to take action before all the information has been collected. In many situations, waiting too patiently for all the facts is to manage by default, to let others make the key decisions, to accept whatever the luck of the draw offers you. It is obvious that not making a decision in time is actually making a decision. There are times to pray and contemplate, to negotiate and compromise to win the best good for the most people, but there are also times to strike when the iron is hot. When some opportunities are past, they are gone forever.

Many years ago when I was in college teaching, I taught a counseling course for pastors in an extension program. The three of us who were teaching off campus each Saturday morning were initially surprised to find ourselves sleeping Friday nights and teaching the next day in an incredible mansion. It had facings of Carrara marble flecked with gold, ancient Persian carpets, cut-glass chandeliers, and much more.

The mansion had been offered to the congregation that sponsored the program for community pastors by a family no longer needing the building. The church bought it for pennies on the dollar, and the sellers got a good tax write-off. The deal had to be made virtually overnight, however, and several key members of the congregation did not want to hurry into the purchase. The pastor quickly bypassed them and used his own property to secure a modest loan until the congregation had time to think the matter through. His courage saved the opportunity, and in a very short time the congregation decided to sell their old building and build a new sanctuary, compatible with the mansion, on the lawn of the great house. The complex then became the best and most-admired education unit, fellowship building, and extension center within the city of several hundred thousand people. This all happened because a pastor with a basically Supporting personality pattern knew how to act as a Controller when such a shift in leadership methods was warranted. Pastor Thompson told me one morning, "It could have blown up in my face if someone in the congregation was gunning for my scalp, but I thought it was crucial to strike while the iron was hot."

The ability to make sound decisions is never inherited like the color of your hair or eyes. It develops, instead, as you mature in leadership ability and the use of facts. If you have the traits that place you on the left of the chart—as a Comprehender or a Supporter, preferring to *ask* people rather than *tell* them—you may find it difficult to take risks about confronting others or in competing with them interpersonally. Had Pastor Thompson followed his normal Supporter instincts to gain a consensus before moving to acquire the mansion, it would have been lost to the congregation forever.

Plan on taking the risks that come naturally to the people on the "compete" side of the chart when the rewards are worth it. Act swiftly when it is appropriate and preach sermons that challenge the people to be bold with you. Tell your congregation where they should stand on vital issues and what they can do to make the work succeed. Use the potential-problem-analysis method I presented in the previous chapter to avoid unnecessary mistakes and then move boldly like a Controller to a successful conclusion of the project.

Setting Objectives

Surely you have learned (by the time you were old enough to read this book) that personal success most often comes from making and carrying out the best possible decisions in most of your activities. Sound decision making is crucial to working effectively and efficiently. If you are effective in your leadership, you have been choosing the right things to do. Perhaps, in your situation, it has been more effective to spend part of your educational budget on a training course to help teachers improve their classroom skills rather than buying new furniture for the rooms. You have seen the increased interest in church school and an increase in average attendance in the upper grades as the youngsters respond to better teaching.

While being effective means that you choose sound objectives, being efficient means that you are making good with those decisions. You are doing the right things in the right way by persuading people to work with you, to follow the feedback methods developed in previous chapters, and so on. It is important to be both effective and efficient, but the top priority is choosing the right things to do, according to management expert Peter Drucker.

Not long ago a pastor friend of mine was in my home for dinner with his wife. To the annoyance of the ladies, we spent too much time discussing shop. Before they stopped us, however, we had a good gossip session about ministers we know and have known in the past. I brought up the name Edward Williams, who had just retired after entering the ministry during World War II. I held him up as a successful parish minister, but my friend pointed out a number of facts about his work. Edward, he said, found himself squarely in front of the post-war suburban juggernaut:

> Ed couldn't fail unless he stole from the treasury and ran off with the choir director. He took what was really a rural church, settled in as the men returned from the war, married, and started the baby boom. Within a few years the fields around the church were covered with housing tracts, shopping centers, and schools. The United States rode the post-war boom, so there was money to burn.

> Men joined his church who had been captains, majors, and colonels. They went to work and made the church a real power in the community. At one time there were so many kids there they had to run three church-school sessions every Sunday. He was at the right place at the right time, and if you don't agree, look how the

church lost half its membership in his last few years there when
the kids grew up and moved away.

Sometimes luck is more important than innate ability, and I
had to agree with my friend: Ed would have had a hard time
failing. Yet I can drive just a few miles from my home to find
another congregation in an even more affluent suburb that
never got it all together. They have been around as long as Ed's
group but never accomplished much of anything. When they
built a church complex, the people found an isolated, tucked-
away location that seemed to symbolize their desire to be left to
themselves. After their children went off to college and married
to set up housekeeping elsewhere, the ranks became thin
through attrition.

Not only could they have grown, like Ed's congregation, to
offer many services to the community, they had another chance
for making it big just a few years ago. One of the strong congregations of our community outgrew its facilities and built six
or seven miles away. Events have shown that fully a third of the
people in the neighborhood chose not to move with the departing
church. Several of us went to the pastor of the ingrown congregation with a plan for his group to buy the buildings no more
than a mile away. He kept asking for more time to consider. The
moment finally passed and another congregation bought the
property. This group has great enthusiasm for God's work, inherited close to five hundred people, and has flourished ever
since. The first group keeps on dwindling because its objectives
were hazy and its leadership indecisive.

Objective pastoral leadership has always been as much of an
art as a science. Nevertheless, leading according to specific,
well-defined objectives allows you to identify what you expect
from your inputs and to plan for appropriate feedback from the
people who are working toward mutual goals. Leading a congregation with a Controller's style enables a pastor to choose a
broader range of opportunities. You can assess each contrib-
utor's potential for success and his or her rate of spiritual
growth. Most important, by leading a parish objectively, you can
decide where to invest resources and relationships so as to do the
most for the church. You can eliminate a great deal of guesswork
by firmly fixing objectives in mind and then teaching your

people how to reach them. It has not been accidental that many modern businesses work through management-by-objectives, although they have found such an approach is not a panacea. Thoughtful leaders know there is no foolproof plan in the work of any organization.

In the previous chapter I wrote that a problem can be considered a deviation from an established base line of performance. To pursue that concept further, consider the fact that much of your work is devoted to maintaining the status quo of smoothly operating subgroups within the congregation. Perhaps you have learned the old management quip, "If it ain't broke, don't fix it." Don't abandon worthwhile and effective methods just because they have been around for some time. Every good sports coach tells his or her team to keep on doing the things that bring success until the other team stops them. Nevertheless, failure to hold on to the past is not much of a problem within the church!

We are more ideological than utopian in our expectations for the church. It is almost as if Christians have been programmed to conserve the best from the past until it turns completely sour. After all, we seem to say, if our faith and practices are from God, they must be universal and eternal. Of course, God *is* eternal and there are elements to Christianity that cannot change without destroying our religion—the incarnation, the resurrection, the gift of the Spirit, the individual priesthood of believers, and the rest. But we people of the church itself do have a temptation to be so conservative that we ignore many good things that can be created through change. We like to cast our traditions and practices in concrete, with convenient handles and catchwords for ease of transmission, and give them to our children and grandchildren so they can use them unchallenged and unexamined. This approach has not worked for a hundred years and probably will never be successful again. The relationship of the church to the rest of society has shifted too much in the last century for that. You will have to go beyond any status quo as society changes with the speed of a whirlwind.

Even pastors who are successful in their leadership—conserving the best from the past according to their understanding of Scripture, reason, experience, and tradition—are efficient in their use of the new. Pat Robertson with his Christian Broadcast Network and Jerry Falwell with his Liberty Baptist complex

use state-of-the-art knowledge about the production of programs, the marketing of ideas, and the financing of projects. You
will have to decide what is best for your congregation by using
the best of the present and future to conserve what is worth
saving from the past.

Types of Decisions

Effective choices occur more often in a pastor's career when he
or she combines verifiable facts, good judgment, and an en-
lightened self-interest. Sound choices are usually made at three
levels in a parish: holding decisions, mitigating decisions, and
corrective decisions.

Holding Decisions. A parish leader will normally use holding decisions in an emergency. They are especially useful in
times of stress to cope with an unexpected deviation from an
established base line. A holding decision is usually appropriate
to avoid a disaster, to buy time until pastor and people can keep
things from falling apart. At such a time it is useless to debate
who is at fault, why the problem occurred, or how much rain is
falling through the roof. You must do something immediately to
solve the problem as a good Controller does. You want a holding
decision to be of as good quality as possible, but it must give you
time to make a possibly better choice later.

If you find your church basement filling with water at two in
the morning, you must access the congregation's telephone tree
to call out the troops. The men and boys can fill and stack sand-
bags to divert the water from a flooding creek. The women can
mop up the water inside. The people are being used to win the
time needed to make a long-term decision when you have more
information about the flood.

Mitigating Decisions. These choices are largely used to
lessen the damage caused by a problem or a potential problem.
Circumstances that are beyond human control often require
mitigating decisions. If water from the creek is flooding the
basement, you or the official board can do little immediately to
control it. The congregation, as with a holding decision, can
move supplies and equipment that the water would ruin. Perhaps a truck can be rented to move supplies and equipment, or
men and women can be called in from neighboring churches to

help. If part of the basement area has been used for meetings or other church-related activities, decisions will have to be made regarding substitute facilities until the area is usable again. Ruined supplies may have to be replaced promptly.

Such mitigating decisions will save supplies and equipment, of course, but will do little to prepare the church for worship on Sunday or keep the disaster from occurring again.

Corrective Decisions. With these decisions we identify the problem and search for causes, so the problem can be kept from occurring again. When your church flooded, you had to wait for the creek waters to subside before suggesting a corrective plan of action to the congregational leaders.

To discover the nature of the decision needed, you will have to do some important research. A visit to the library may show that the creek has never flooded before in recorded history. In that case you may want to chance it and do nothing at all. On the other hand, your research may reveal that a city upstream on the creek has recently tied its storm drains into the main channel. Every heavier-than-average rain will cause trouble in the future. Obviously you will have to make a decision about chronic flooding.

Your investigation may reveal several choices you can make. The congregation might persuade city and state officials to build an earthen dam to control the runoff. The church property would then be protected. Perhaps a park could be built by the lake created by the dam, increasing the value of the church's property. You may have to initiate a law suit to block the use of the creek by the upstream city. Possibly an injunction could be secured until the case is settled in court. The congregation may have to build a dike alongside its property to hold the water from the building. But, in each case, the congregational leaders are working on corrective measures. They have gone to the heart of the matter and will do something about it.

Unfortunately, people in leadership positions often misunderstand the kinds of decisions they make. They confuse holding or mitigating decisions with corrective choices. When that happens, the final result solves nothing and often makes matters worse. More serious problems arise because the time that could have been used to develop a corrective decision has been wasted.

People may become complacent with a patchwork decision and stop trying to find a corrective choice for the overall problem.

I believe this is what happened regarding sexuality within the Roman Catholic Church. As a worldwide civilization of Christians and non-Christians, we have come to understand that legitimate sexual expression is a normal adjunct to married love. No more than a minute handful of people see sexual relations as the original sin or as a carnal weakness that God condones in order to produce children. Few ordinary people accept such a medieval concept, which did not even develop in the church for a thousand years after the Scriptures were written. The normal condition for church pastors for ten centuries was marriage, conjugal pleasure, and rearing children.

Unfortunately for the Roman Catholic congregations, their young men and women agree in large numbers with the non-Catholic view of sound sexuality. The church has had a tremendous falling off of candidates for the priesthood and the religious orders. Research places this decline squarely in the area of lifelong celibacy, as can be seen in the flood of non-Catholic candidates for the ministry in various denominations.

The decision made by the Roman Catholic hierarchy seems to me to be a mitigating one, whereas the need is for a corrective choice. The church's leaders refuse to acknowledge that their view of sexual love cannot be substantiated by Scripture, early church theology and tradition, or by contemporary psychology. They choose to maintain the status quo that came from medieval theologians, who were probably quite neurotic by any modern mental-health standard. The Catholic hierarchy has organized teams of priests and nuns to beat the bushes of their communities to recruit youngsters to a celibate life. Every once in a while, they find such a young man or woman, but they are the first to admit that the going is tough. By using a mitigating decision rather than a corrective one, this church could well find itself with half as many priests and nuns as it needs within another decade or two. Apparently no one in the Vatican has done a potential problem analysis of what could happen should they continue to consider human sexuality in medieval concepts into the next generation.

Figure 22 **Decision-Making Process**

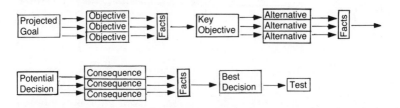

The Decision-Making Process

Assume that you are the senior pastor of a church that has a staff of four full-time ministers and twelve other men and women in different positions. When you are on vacation in Wisconsin, you discover how smoothly the church school functions in a congregation pastored by an old seminary friend. There seems to be none of the confusion, noise, and disruptive horseplay and lack of attention you find distasteful in your home parish. When you and your friend discuss it during a round of golf, you are surprised to find that his church school functions with more children than your own congregation. When you arrive home, you decide to reorganize your own educational program so as to make the most of the time and talent available— but you don't know precisely where to begin.

To use my decision-making process, work from the beginning to the end, as you did with the problem-solving process in the previous chapter. The flow is outlined in figure 22.

To use the decision-making process correctly, enter your anticipated goal in the box at the far left. In this case it is "smooth church school" (see figure 23).

Even if you are basically a Controller, you realize that little will be accomplished unless everyone on the staff cooperates and that each worker knows his or her job better than you know it. You hold a staff meeting and use the skills that would come naturally to a Comprehender to gather and analyze facts and

Figure 23 **Projected Goal**

> Smooth
> Church
> School

Figure 24 **Objectives**

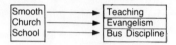

information. All suggestions are written on a flip chart to keep unpleasant or seemingly unimportant facts from being lost in the give-and-take you know will come from your opinionated and articulate men and women.

As the discussion gets under way, some precise objectives arise. For example, your religious-education director and the coordinator of volunteers believes that much of the disruption occurs because the volunteer teachers lack the type of training in educational practices that professional teachers receive. One group works hard and wants to teach well, but simply doesn't know enough about child psychology and teaching principles to do much more than lecture. The children become restless. Another group, the coordinator of volunteers reports, has its hands full dealing with the junior-high group. None of these kids seems willing to talk seriously to adults, perhaps because the materials do not seem relevant to them.

Your minister of evangelism immediately counters by saying that the church school needs to develop an improved system for bringing new families into the church school, to use them as a feeder for the church itself. It is her contention that, with new blood, the church school will be more interesting to everyone involved.

Several of the office staff report that they feel the kids are arriving overly excited and ready to keep playing because the bus drivers allow them to run wild on the bus. They come into the church more inclined to tear around than to study or discuss the lesson of the day.

As the ideas are presented and relevant information selected, several objectives appear. These are plotted on the chart as in figure 24.

The facts that emerge reveal that virtually everyone on your staff feels that certain changes need to be made to improve the hour of instruction. These are the facts you will use to evaluate the individual objectives. Enter these on the flip chart (see figure 25).

Figure 25 **Facts**

As you discuss the problem further, a key objective seems to appear. Teachers, bus drivers and Sunday-school callers all appear poorly equipped to succeed at their tasks. You plot the immediate objective in the appropriate box (figure 26) as "better performance." Note that you have temporarily "ignored" the evangelism issue as a priority, although it obviously has some bearing on the overall problem. As a good leader, you will no doubt consider this in the near future.

You next talk about the general need for improved performance and ask for suggestions about reaching such a goal. The people are quick to tell you their feelings. "I want better people in the classrooms," the education director tells you. "Can't we find enough professional teachers to work with our kids on Sunday?" You enter that suggestion. The volunteer director tells you that he wants more people to keep order in the halls and between the education center and the sanctuary. You also plot that on your chart. Your secretary admits the importance of the previous suggestions but tells how the previous church in which she worked solved most of its church-school problems with a two-year-long training program for various workers. You sigh— Ah ha!—and plot that also (figure 27).

As the discussion continues and you and the others examine the alternatives, you become aware of several additional facts. You state that from your previous experience it is very difficult to get professional teachers to teach on Sunday. A large percentage of them appear to feel that they have spent enough time with kids during the work week. (One of your associate ministers, who is married to a fifth-grade teacher, tells how he had never been able to persuade his wife to teach in the church school for that reason.) The education director explains that he is not com-

Figure 26 **Immediate Objective**

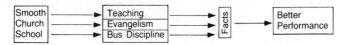

FIGURE 27 **Alternatives and Facts**

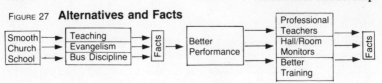

fortable with the idea of putting guards in the halls or monitors in the rooms. "We have them here," he says, "to teach them, to help them learn, not to keep them in chains. I didn't get a masters in RE to become a warden in a juvenile hall," he concludes. All related information and observations are also listed on the chart, under "facts."

The viable alternative appears to be a good training program for different people doing different things in the church school. You want to improve their efficiency. You want them to do the right things with the kids and to do those jobs the best they possibly can. The potential decision, acknowledged by the group, is to train the workers to be the best possible in their relationships with the youngsters—on the busses as the youngsters are on the way to church and in the classrooms and adjoining areas. You realize that even the previously "postponed" evangelism problem seems somewhat mitigated, since better-equipped volunteers will be more highly motivated for outreach and consequently will enroll new youngsters from the community.

You and your staff must also consider the consequences of an extended training program. The chart now looks like figure 28, with a final feedback check or "test" to see how well things are going:

An improved training program will have certain consequences, of course. There may be some resistance to attending classes by the volunteer workers. Some may feel that they are

FIGURE 28 **Complete Decision-Making Chart**

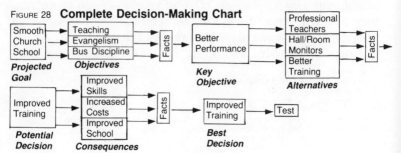

already contributing enough time or that their experience alone qualifies them as good teachers. In that case you shall have to communicate the need for better conditions as "ministry to the children." You may want to make the teaching core an elite group within the church and reward them psychologically and philosophically.

The consequences of a more effective and efficient school can be accepted universally without any great conflict—but you still have to find the finances with which to pay for the training programs. You have a tough finance-committee chairman, but you know a few wealthy people in the community who have always been willing to support the church with several thousand dollars when it was really needed. One is a wealthy automobile dealer who has always supplied the congregation with busses at a fraction of normal costs; another is the owner of a manufacturing firm who has long been active in scouting. When someone asks about the money, you tell them decisively that you can handle it all right. Everyone nods, and the consensus you like has been reached. You will now direct and work with the appropriate people to plan an educational program for autumn. You will want to keep close to it and finally test the program from time to time to see that it remains on track.

Every pastor should pause from time to time to assess the information he or she has and run it through the decision-making process to keep from overlooking problems that may occur. Don't forget to walk your decisions through the potential problem analysis shown in the previous chapter to avoid any unpleasant surprises along the way! Whatever your personal personality pattern, remember to draw on Controlling strengths to make bold decisions when necessary to spur your congregation into worthwhile action toward sound objectives.

7

Inspirational Parish Leadership— Member Coaching

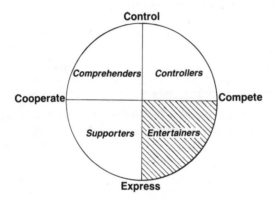

T he men and women who fit in the lower-right quadrant of the Personality Pattern distribution chart are the people I call Entertainers in the Self-Profile. They combine competitive and expressive traits in such a way that they might remind you of comedians Johnny Carson and Joan Rivers as well as President Lyndon Johnson. (You may wish to review chapter four to recall how the people with this pattern react to and relate with others.) Such men and women come across as warm in their relationships, willing to take interpersonal risks with their articulate mannerisms. They are rather talkative, and do not seem as self-controlled as people in the top half of the chart since they are more interested in self-expression.

"How stubborn you are!" Stephen went on to say. "How heathen
your hearts, how deaf you are to God's message! You are just like
your ancestors; you too have always resisted the Holy Spirit! Was
there any prophet that your ancestors did not persecute? They
killed God's messengers, who long ago announced the coming of
his righteous Servant. And now you have betrayed and murdered
him. You are the ones who received God's law, that was handed
down by angels—yet you have not obeyed it!"

Acts 7:51–53

As Stephen did in the above passage of Scripture, people with
the Entertaining pattern use a number of methods to express
their emotions to people. You can just see Stephen standing on
tiptoe, shaking his finger at the scholars as he began *telling
them what he was feeling* about their rejection of the Lord Jesus
Christ.

The traits of Entertainers combine, as do yours and mine,
according to the $P = f(H \times E \times C)$ equation that has appeared
several times before. Remember that each person's pattern is the
function or result of his or her heredity traits being multiplied
by key childhood experiences. That product is multiplied again
by the significant choices the person makes while growing up.

The most obvious strength that an Entertaining-style pastor
brings to God's work in a local parish is a talent to inspire and
motivate people to high achievement. Every pastor needs to
cultivate the ability to create a climate of high expectation and
excitement about the work of the congregation. Entertainers
are typically uncomfortable in situations or relationships where
feelings are squelched in favor of cold logic. Leaders with this
pattern normally want to accomplish the work that needs to be
done but insist that everything accomplished must occur
through people. Therefore, they focus on the people and expect
the work to follow in due course. Entertainers tend to build
relationships more quickly than the Controllers and Comprehenders at the top of the personality diagram, but they are also
capable of abandoning them just as quickly.

I can understand this tendency, for I fit almost dead center in
the Entertaining quadrant of the Personality Pattern chart. I
have found it too easy all my life to go from one city to another
and leave friends behind. There are always new ones out there!
Now that I spend most of my time writing books, I reach a point

from time to time when I must flee from my office to meet people and maintain relationships, which are very important to people with my pattern.

If you will think about it for a moment, it becomes obvious that a pastor who has the verbal and interpersonal ability to inspire and motivate a congregation can be very successful as a leader. Few congregations will prosper without the kind of spiritual excitement that can be generated by people with this Entertaining pattern. Every congregation needs a vision of what can be, and its enthusiasm can be aroused by a person willing to speak out about what they can accomplish as friends working well together.

Borrowing the Entertainer's Strengths

Perhaps the greatest contribution an Entertaining pastor can make to a congregation is his or her ability to coach people to find satisfaction by giving more of themselves to God's work. By capturing the imagination of more and more people and showing them how to work effectively and efficiently, the pastor multiplies his or her impact dramatically. The congregation can become not only a fellowship of believers but also a community of achievers that takes spiritual satisfaction from its accomplishments.

In the pop-entertainment industry, there is a saying that the most technically polished singers are usually relegated to the chorus. I think of Carol Channing and Louis Armstrong especially when I make that statement, but younger readers will have to find their own examples. Real stars have a charisma that transcends actual ability. In other words, people do relate positively to those men and women in the public eye who are able and willing to step out of the crowd, to use their strong interpersonal skills and take the spotlight.

If you do not have an Entertaining pattern, you will have to develop these skills. Every great accomplishment begins as the germ of an idea within someone's mind, grows as it is expressed enthusiastically to others, and comes to fruition only when some leader puts together a team of people who believe the work can be done. Jesus recognized this as he led his disciples, Paul used the principle as he established churches across the civilized world, and so did the pastors I interviewed for my research.

If you are not naturally an Entertainer, you may feel foolish starting to be the congregation's cheerleader. But you probably were also uncomfortable preaching your first sermon. I certainly was. I had two outlines memorized, so I preached the first one and looked at my watch. Since it had taken only eight minutes, gracefully or otherwise, I preached the second outline. Only another eight minutes had passed. (I still carry a watch with me in the pulpit or at the podium but for another reason now!) You probably felt some discomfort at conducting your first wedding or funeral. As you did then, you can also become comfortable as the parish coach.

There is more to this than a simple rah-rah approach, for as I reported in chapter three, men and women are motivated in the physical, psychological, and philosophical aspects of life. People are moved to achieve in the parish only when it becomes personally important to do so. It is only when people have an ownership of the outcome that they will commit themselves to the work. They will not do great things so *you* can be famous in the denomination or be promoted to a more prestigious congregation. They will work when you inspire them to do so and see that they win the rewards of accomplishment.

Striving for Authenticity

When you communicate high expectations and enthusiasm to your members, make a special effort to keep your verbal and your nonverbal communication congruent. Make sure that you are not sending conflicting messages to the people you are trying to influence, because this will create doubt and suspicion. Because we learn to interpret the tone of another voice and body language long before we learn to use words, nonverbal communication will be considered first.

Picture yourself as you join the finance-committee chairman of your congregation in talking to a banker about a loan to build an addition to the building. Imagine, as you present your plans, that the banker stops you to make a phone call for a golf date. After a while, as you are still talking, he turns his chair to stare at the clouds framed by his window. Then his secretary brings in some papers, and he leafs through them to sign and seal each one. What would your reaction be? Even if he told you he would bring the matter before his loan committee, would your expectations be high? Of course not, unless you are so inept in interpersonal relationships that you cannot interpret an insult!

People normally become confused and frightened when someone in authority sends contradictory messages. They almost automatically interpret it as an attempt to deceive them or as a sign that the person sending the conflicting messages has lost control. In parish dealings, neither assumption does a lot of good for the work of the congregation or for the minister's reputation, for that matter. In either case, the listeners will close up to protect themselves and the people they care about.

Another term for congruency or authenticity is emotional honesty. When a minister sends conflicting signals to people, it is seldom a deliberate attempt to deceive. Most of such messages occur because the pastor is out of his comfort zone or in an egocentric predicament because of ambivalent feelings. It happens like this:

A seminary student I heard about was walking down the street with his fiancée. They were chatting comfortably, enjoying the pleasant day, planning some aspect of their coming wedding. As Roy Wooten looked up he saw a man he had long considered one of his best friends. Realizing that the friend and Laura had never met, Roy stopped when the newcomer approached them. He turned to his fiancée, smiled, and said, "I want you to meet one of my best friends." But Roy was horrified to realize he could not remember the man's name. He stammered a bit and decided he had better shift directions and approach the situation from the other way. He decided to introduce his fiancée to his friend but, to his greater horror, discovered he could not recall *her* name! He felt as you or I would have—a complete idiot—as he muttered some absurd apology and dragged Laura away by the arm.

It was not until they were alone on a park bench that Roy puzzled through his egocentric predicament. Convention, custom, and good manners demanded a polite introduction of Laura to the friend. But it had been that very friend who, when Roy had introduced a previous girl friend to him at a party, had wooed her away from him. Unconsciously, without the past event being considered at the time, Roy's ego protected itself by blocking another introduction to the man. As Roy and Laura unraveled the cause of his apparently illogical ambivalent feelings, they made sense. For a moment, however, she had wondered whether he was trying to deceive her about something or losing his grip on reality.

Facets of Emotional Honesty

Practice the following to keep people listening to you:

Remain emotionally honest (authentic).

Accept all emotions as legitimate.

Reveal your emotions when appropriate.

Remain Emotionally Honest. To be authentic in your relationships, you must learn to recognize what you are feeling. And, while I wish I could state that this is easy, the truth is that it is often quite difficult. As flawed humans, we all tend to place the best possible explanations on our emotions and relationships. We rationalize our feelings. Less noble people than I may be angry, but *I* feel righteous indignation when something or someone frustrates me. *I* feel a holy love, but another person feels sinful lust. *I* protect my good name, but you insult people needlessly. Excuse-making behavior is normal within limits as we try to remain in our comfort zone, but it gets out of hand with some ministers and lay people alike. We have all heard variations of the little boy's lament, "The fight started when he pushed me back."

I know a minister (who will remain nameless to protect the guilty) who has made a career out of lambasting a major denomination from his extended-community church complex. He rants and raves repeatedly at how "they" are dupes of Satan, international Communism, and the Zionists, who control international banking. There seems to be no limit to the hostility he can summon up to belabor the group he dislikes so intensely. The fascinating thing, however, is that he was once determined to become a pastor in that denomination and would have, if he had not flunked his Minnesota Multiphasic Personality Inventory. His paranoia was off-scale, and they turned him down. He went out on his own, built a congregation with conspiracy buffs like himself, and now has a made-to-order pulpit for lashing out at those who would not accept him twenty years ago. No doubt he has found a way to justify his revenge.

When a frightened secretary confesses that she has failed to mail in on time the application for a seminar you wanted to attend, you probably will not lash out at her. Neither can you honestly tell her that it's all right if your eyelid is flickering, your temple vein throbbing, and your face red with anger. She sees that and interprets it before she hears your soothing words. In fact, she will probably not believe any words that contradict your nonverbal communication. If you will lay aside the mistaken assumption or the absurd belief that you never become angry or that people force it on you, be emotionally honest with yourself and her. Admit that she has messed up your plans and that you resent it. She already knows that, and the only person you fool with deception is yourself.

Accept Emotions as Legitimate. You can accept your feelings if you have the maturity to recognize all human emotions as legitimate and natural. They are "normal" in that they have survival characteristics. To be so frightened that your voice squeaks and your hands shake is normal in a hurricane regardless of your personal commitment to Christ and your spiritual maturity. To be angry when a bully humiliates you, and to take steps so he or she does not humiliate you further, is as natural as a mother's love for her child. (Don't ever let anyone tell you that being a pastor is a life of quiet contemplation. It can be a battleground!) Normal men and women, who have not been repressed or traumatized, will feel sexual desire and be attracted to interesting people of the opposite sex. All of the above, and many other legitimate emotions, must be regulated and guided in accord with one's values and beliefs.

I have never seen it as an advantage for a pastor to attack a member with a volley of verbal abuse because the person had frustrated some plan—nor to run screaming from a committee meeting because something was not going right. In a civilized world such as the church claims to personify, our emotions must be refined and used appropriately.

Reveal your emotions when appropriate. In the case of

the negligent secretary who failed to make your seminar reservation, you could and should say something like this:

> Of course I'm angry about the mistake. I had made my plans to attend and now will have to revise everything. I'm going to miss a program that would have been important to the church. Naturally, I don't want such carelessness again. If you must, make a list of the things that must be done and check them off. I feel very strongly about this and expect your cooperation. If you need help, talk to me.

You have been emotionally honest in saying what your nonverbal body language and tone of voice have already revealed to her, coached her in a suggestion to follow, and invited some feedback. You never made a personal attack on her motives or intelligence, but have expressed your feelings in an appropriate manner.

Coaching with Correction

I have reached a point in my counseling and lecturing career wherein I cringe when I hear someone in a leadership position speak of "constructive criticism." I no longer believe that anyone in a subordinate position gains anything from *any* kind of criticism. In fact, I suspect that the vast bulk of criticism of others is nothing more than an attempt to return to the critic's comfort zone and assure himself that he was not at fault. All kinds of criticism trigger such resistance and resentment from the recipient that it is wisest to say nothing and then start a correction process.

Here is how the wrong scenario would go: Wally Burns, a driver and assistant custodian for the parish, has hit another vehicle and ruined a fender on one of the church busses. The associate pastor in charge of religious education and transportation catches him in the garage.

Associate: (Loudly) For heaven's sake, Wally, you've been driving a church bus long enough to watch out for traffic. Why don't you go to driving school if you can't drive? Idiot!

Wally: (Defensively) It was only a fender-bender.

FIGURE 29 **Criticism-Conflict Pattern**

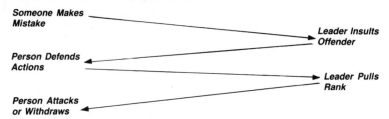

Associate: Fender-bender! Baloney! You've always been care-less around here. What you need is to be penalized some way for your goof-ups. I'm going to speak to the trustees about getting you back in line.

Wally: I couldn't see her in my blind spot. I've been asking for new mirrors for weeks, and no one has done anything about it. If you had gotten me the mirrors like I wanted, there would have been no accident.

Associate: That's enough of that right now! *You* have an acci-dent and want to blame *me* for your stupidity? I'm going to have you up in front of the trustees and let you explain your carelessness to them.

Wally gulps hard, remembering the fight he had with the trustees for his raise and the criticism one made about his failure to clean the kitchen properly after a youth dinner. He keeps his mouth shut but his brain is racing. Although he returns to work, he has a desire to prove to someone that he is not a patsy to be pushed around so easily. He may start using his sick days unnecessarily and take advantage of the staff whenever possible.

The associate pastor has turned a simple accident, which is covered by insurance and resulted in no injuries, into a conflict that was never necessary. If this is the pattern used by the associate when things go wrong, the relationship between church leadership and the employees and volunteers may follow the sequence shown in figure 29.

Try not to deal with the one responsible for a mistake or accident immediately after it has occurred, if at all possible. The person who has blundered already feels like an idiot, is probably in an egocentric predicament, and is too tense to listen to criticism or even to correction. Never confuse criticism with correction. The associate could have spoken to Wally like this:

> *Associate:* (Calmly) That's quite a crunch. Glad no one was hurt.
>
> *Wally:* I'll be the first to admit that.
>
> *Associate:* We'll have to get estimates and report to the insurance company. What went wrong?
>
> *Wally:* Those darned old mirrors have lost their clarity. I didn't see her coming up until I started my turn.
>
> *Associate:* You could have looked, however?
>
> *Wally:* Yeah, I really goofed, but I would have missed her with good mirrors.
>
> *Associate:* I'll get them, but you promise me you'll look behind you in the future.
>
> *Wally:* All right, and thanks.

Because the associate pastor was coaching Wally rather than criticizing him, the driver thanked him—for not making a big issue of a crumpled fender and promising to get some needed equipment. Both men can feel good about themselves and about their settling of the problem.

Rules for Coaching People

As you work with church employees and the members, make a determined effort to put trivial events and crucial mistakes in proper perspective. A collapsed music stand in the Christmas cantata is not as important as an earthquake-weakened roof. An unhappy woman who complains that you should be more dignified when playing on the church softball team probably represents no one but herself in the criticism. You want to keep such things in proportion so other people will, too. Then they will commit themselves to matters of importance and spend less time and effort on things that are not.

I recommend five principles that a good pastoral coach should follow most of the time:

Remain as congruent as possible.

Avoid threats, bluffs, and psychological games.

Carefully emphasize potential modifiers.

Avoid nagging and sarcasm.

Lead by your own best example.

Remain Congruent. Be authentic and emotionally honest, although you will have good days and bad days as you work through the congregation. Your attitudes will shift somewhat according to your moods, biorhythms, and possibly the phases of the moon. These shifts must not be permitted to lessen your ability to work with the people of the parish. As I suggested above, do your best to send your messages without the conflicting elements that cause people to think you are trying to deceive them or that you are losing self-control. Work at recognizing your feelings in different situations, accept them as normal, and share them with others when it is right to do so.

Avoid Threats, Bluffs, Psychological Games. The use of such challenges and devices are unworthy of a pastor, of course. In addition, in our era of shared authority and responsibility, you seldom have the power to use them. People will leave you to do the work by yourself, and the congregation holds the collective power to advance or hinder your career. People can go the second mile because they want to help you or they can force you to drag the work along as best you can. Since psychological weapons are used to set people up for pain, they have no place in your work.

Emphasize Potential Modifiers. You must take great care to make sure your promises are carried out. It is better to keep quiet on what you plan to do until you see the objective and outcome clearly. Remember that it can be very harmful to raise expectations and then not reach your goals, even though changing circumstances are not your fault. Spell out in advance any possible pitfalls that may change the outcome and keep things low key until ready to move ahead successfully.

Avoid Nagging and Sarcasm. Once you have coached a person with adequate training and are sure it is understood, repeating the instructions over and over will merely show that you don't trust the individual. Your coaching through correction

FIGURE 30 **ASRAC Coaching Process**

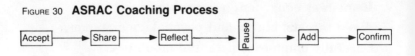

should deal with tasks and goals and ignore motives, commitment, and personalities as much as possible. Sarcasm is cruel
and evil and has no place in helping people do the work of the
church in a more effective manner.

Lead by Your Own Best Example. This is one of the key
factors I found in my research about leadership in successful,
growing congregations. Good leaders always exemplify the values, attitudes, expectations, beliefs, and choices that make a
congregation do great things. I think of John Wesley, the peri-
patetic pastor who covered England for decades on horseback to
build strong parishes. It has been said that when he died he left
behind virtually nothing *but* the Methodist Church.

The Coaching Process

This process will let you do several things. First, it allows the
person being coached to gain emotional relief from any confusion or embarrassment at being corrected for a mistake. Next,
the process also allows the user to understand the other person's
motives. He can tell you what he feels about the situation. Finally, you can use the process to make corrections in such a way
that the person agrees with you to carry out your suggestions. Of
course, you must always remember that no technique or process
will allow you to manipulate people without their recognizing
who is humiliating or using them. Figure 30 outlines the five
steps of ASRAC, the coaching process.

Imagine that you are in a setting where one of your youth
leaders seems incapable of maintaining order in the scout troop
that meets on Tuesday evenings in your social hall. After several
parents complain that a few inconsiderate and troublesome
youngsters are disrupting everything, you investigate the situation before jumping to conclusions and fixing something not yet
broken. You discover that the scoutmaster either ignores the
disruptive boys for too long or grows angry and sends them
home. You are not satisfied with either choice for the leader,

Figure 31 **Acceptance**

| Accept |

because one response keeps the entire group from gaining satisfaction while the other does nothing to correct the troublemakers.

You begin using the ASRAC coaching process by calling the scoutmaster in for a discussion. Perhaps it would be best to keep it informal by inviting him to breakfast or lunch at a nearby restaurant. As you talk about the problem, you speak in an emotionally honest manner by telling him you want to help him become the best leader he can be. You begin the discussion by asking him to tell you his view of the situation. As he does, you accept whatever he has to say (see figure 31).

Accept without reservation, self-defense, interruption, or criticism everything the scout leader talks about. Accept all that he says, even if he is criticizing your theology, most-cherished traditions, pastoral style, or the memory of your sacred mother. Encourage him to tell you what is on his mind about the youngsters, their parents, the problems caused by a few, and anything else that comes up, even if it seems irrelevant. You must accept his emotions or you will shut him off and never learn what you need to know to coach him successfully. Listen acceptingly so as to get into his mind and emotions and have him open up to you.

Demonstrate the fact that you are listening supportively by maintaining a positive nonverbal attitude. Have your body language and tone of voice demonstrate your acceptance of him as a worthwhile person, even when he says things with which you cannot agree. To show your acceptance of him, nod from time to time or say something like, "That's an interesting point," or "Tell me more about that," or "I understand where you're coming from."

By listening acceptingly, you do two key things. You offer the speaker a catharsis he would never receive otherwise, and you gather information you would not receive if you were to criticize his statements or dominate the situation. Keep a sense of purpose in mind, for you are not meeting with the scout leader to demonstrate your brilliance or your power. When he has nothing

FIGURE 32 **Sharing**

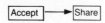

more to say, go to the following part of the coaching process (figure 32).

Sharing the scout leader's emotions will demonstrate your concern better than anything else you can do at this point. Share by putting yourself in his place. Realize that he is young, eager to succeed in his work for the congregation, and fearful of failing. Go back to the concerns you heard by listening and say, when appropriate, something like this: "Having the paint spilled must have frustrated you badly." "I've also felt like giving it all up with difficult kids." "I've never found it easy to corral a bunch of yahoos either."

When you have the scout leader's attention because you have shared authentically with him, move on to the next part of the process (figure 33).

The best way to reflect a person's statements and emotions accurately is to paraphrase them, as Carl Rogers taught in client-centered counseling. You can begin by saying something like:

> Tell me if I'm understanding you here. Do you mean to say that you enjoy scouting, but the effort of maintaining control of the rowdy ones is destroying your commitment to the others? Is that what you're telling me?

Of course it is—for you have put into words what his verbal and nonverbal communication have revealed. Any person with a modicum of understanding and patience can reflect another's emotions like this, but the sad fact is that virtually no one ever does except for a professional counselor. By reflecting *his* feelings, *you* appear an interpersonal genius, and he will listen carefully for the following reason: a considerable body of collected research reveals that people are more likely to do what we

FIGURE 33 **Reflecting**

FIGURE 34 **Pause and Add**

ask of them when they believe their feelings are understood. If you will accept another's emotions, share his feelings with him, and demonstrate understanding by reflecting those feelings, you convey knowledge and wisdom in such a way that he will want to follow your suggestions.

There is an emotional break in the coaching process after the first three steps. In coaching others, most people go right to the facts—and that's wrong! You should first deal with feelings, as I have done above, and deal with facts later. The understanding of facts and the act of conveying that understanding is so important that I will use another paraphrased example to make it clear. The "pause" will allow time for clarification, for example:

> Let me get this straight, if you don't mind. Go right ahead and correct me if I've missed the point. Is that all right with you? Are you saying that your problems controlling those kids come because their parents have turned them loose? Is that what you've told me?

Now, go on with the facts you want him to consider (figure 34). Begin dealing with facts by adding information for him to use in working with the boys. These facts can be new to him or they can be familiar concepts that you present in a new way. You pause for a moment and then remember that several teachers in the church school have complained of having discipline problems—in fact, with some of the same youngsters who are disrupting scouting operations. You take this opportunity to do something you have been mulling around for some time. You add new information:

> Thank you for being so frank with me. I understand your problem much better now and have something I would like to have you consider. A number of our teachers have the same problem with discipline. So does the youth minister on her outings. The problem is obviously broader than the scout meetings alone. I'm going to organize a youth- and child-workers discussion setting that

FIGURE 35 **Confirming**

will meet for an hour every month until we get this ironed out. Charles Dunning is a school psychologist who would help, and Mary Rush is a social-worker child specialist. Some of the more experienced teachers can tell how they mastered class discipline without humiliating the children or making them lose their enthusiasm for coming here. How does this strike you?

The scoutmaster will have to come to the meetings for a few nights, but you have moved to get him the coaching needed to become outstanding so far as discipline is concerned. You have added something new as a means of dealing with the facts of the situation. You are offering him the opportunity of feeling better about his contributions to the parish. Then go to the final coaching step (figure 35).

You ask him to make a commitment to confirm his acceptance of your suggestion. Winning a commitment keeps the issue from coming up again, for he will recall it as an agreement to be fulfilled. Ask him to confirm the arrangement:

> When would you like to start the discussion groups? We have a full month before Easter, so we could begin soon. Or if you prefer, we could wait until the following month for the sessions to start. Which would you prefer?

If you will take the time to coach a member or even a church employee in this manner, the process becomes very effective. You come to grips with his or her confusion and uncertainties, show your understanding and support, demonstrate a desire to help in concrete ways, and set up a growth experience that cannot be gracefully refused. In our example, you have made it easy for this young man to accept the opportunity to mature as a scout leader. He will be part of a fully competent group in the parish's community of achievers.

If you will borrow the skills that come naturally to an Entertainer, it matters not what your instinctive pattern is. You will be able to lead other people with enthusiasm and coach them to be more effective and efficient in doing God's work. At first, working with people in this manner may seem to take more time than just giving them instructions. But it requires a great deal less time in the long run, for you will have to fight brush fires less and less often.

8

Supportive Parish Leadership—
Member Counseling

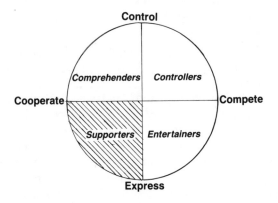

The people who fit in the lower-left sector of the Personality Pattern distribution chart are the ones I call Supporters in the Self-Profile. They combine expressive and cooperative traits in such a way that they remind you of actor Glenn Ford, singer Dinah Shore, and President Ronald Reagan. (You may find it helpful to turn back to chapter four to refresh your understanding of people with Supporting patterns and how they relate to others.) Supporters come across as warmly people-oriented. They are more interested in seeing the work accomplished through happy people rather than through men and women who are competitively driven to achieve. They avoid in-

terpersonal risks that leave others hurt and feel that cooperation is better than competition. Supporters can be considered
the agreement experts of life. They tend to be concerned with
how others feel, whatever the situation.

> [Jesus said:] "And if someone takes you to court to sue you for
> your shirt, let him have your coat as well. And if one of the occupa-
> tion troops forces you to carry his pack one mile, carry it two
> miles. When someone asks you for something, give it to him;
> when someone wants to borrow something, lend it to him."
>
> Matthew 5:40–42

If I had to make an unscientific guess about the role that
ministers prefer to assume, I would suspect that most would like
to be thought of as Supporters in their relationships. As I said
about Entertainers (across the vertical line from this position)
Supporters tend to accept their own emotions, although they are
not so dramatic about expressing them. Rather than reveal what
they feel, they tend to inquire about the feelings of others. To
remain in their comfort zones, they more often *ask others what
they are feeling*.

As occurs with all four primary patterns, a Supporter's style
of interaction develops according to the personality equation
shown several times previously. Following their orientation toward agreement in relationships, Supporters automatically and
instinctively try to deal with the feelings that others bring to
different situations. They assume that they can operate best
when they call upon the cooperative skills needed to get things
done with a minimum of hurt feelings and resentment in an
organization.

Supporters are often uncomfortable with people who are
brusk and abrupt, controllers and comprehenders, for example,
who are so task-oriented that they ignore the fact that all work is
done through people. In contrast, Supporters rarely remain cool
and impersonal in their relationships. Because they are often
introspective and willing to take time to discuss ramifications of
group decisions and choices, they may appear ineffectual to fast-
acting people. They may be fond of such clichés as "You are never
given time to do the work right the first time, but there is always
time enough to do it right the second time."

Outer-limit Supporters at the fringe of the behavioral distribution may be too placid and "cooperative," too unwilling to give instructions and orders to become a good parish leader. There comes a time in every minister's life and work when he or she must stop deliberating the choices still open and get off the starting line. Assignments must be made and people told to get the work done on schedule. About one-fourth of all pastors have a Supporting pattern, although more assume they do. Roughly the same proportion of all church members have it also.

If you will think about it for a moment, you will realize that a pastor who approaches congregational leadership from such a cooperative and feeling-oriented position can be very successful, especially in winning the trust of his members. Few churches will prosper without the supporting-and-developing patterns that come naturally to Supporters. Every congregation needs a leader with the ability to counsel men and women to be at their best in a variety of ways. Every parish needs a pastor who can heal wounds and turn aside conflicts without surrendering the principles of spirituality.

Borrowing the Supporter's Strengths

By learning how to use counseling and negotiating skills, which Supporters use especially well without thinking about them, any pastor can become a better leader. You can support your people as they struggle to fulfill their physical, psychological, and philosophical needs. Few congregations will become strong in spirituality and outreach without the leadership and guidance of people who use strong counseling skills to help the members mature in worship and service.

A major strength of the most successful pastors I met while researching this book proved to be their ability to empathize with and understand the pain that others were suffering. Although God remains unchanging and Christ's message is eternal, temporal life is filled with changes both good and bad. Anyone who assumes that a Christian life locks one into a rigid lifestyle, or that there is only one pattern for spiritual growth, is sadly mistaken. Life and the very rhythms of the universe are based on change.

Just recently I met an elderly woman who has suffered paralysis and is confined to a wheelchair in a nursing home. As we

talked and I tried to counsel her, it seemed that all she did was
blame God for her condition. She kept saying, "How could God
turn on me so? I served him all my life and claimed the promises
of the Scripture that he would care for me. Why has he abandoned me like this?" I tried to counsel her by telling her that
being a Christian never exempts us from suffering, guilt, and
death. This woman must have moved through life without being
aware of the suffering of the people in her congregation. She
must have expected God to give her a magical mystery cure that
would exempt her from the troubles that Job experienced.

I later discussed her confusion about how life must be lived
and her resentment about her existence with one of my pastors.
And, while I take no credit for it, a short time later he preached a
marvelous sermon titled "When the Seagull Doesn't Come." It
was based on the experiences of Captain Eddie Rickenbacker in
World War II, when he and his crew were forced down in mid-
Pacific by engine failure in their B-17. They drifted for days,
suffering horribly from exposure to excessive sunlight, from a
lack of food, and especially from being without water. When
things were at their worst, a seagull flapped up to the rubber
raft and landed on a crewman's shoulders. He reached up very
carefully, grabbed the bird by the legs, and killed it. The men ate
the flesh and drank the blood and thereby survived until rescued. The crew were filled with praise of God for performing a
miracle for their benefit, and one wrote a book about it.

In the sermon, my pastor acknowledged that God does bless
us from time to time—even continually—but if we expect a simple one-to-one payoff for our faith and worship, what happens
when the seagull doesn't come? For every downed air crew that
survived through a miracle, a hundred or more drifted on to
their deaths. Did God love them less? Not at all. My elderly
friend was never rescued in this life, for she died last week. She
was loved no less than anyone else by God, and I hope my counseling helped her through the last great difficulties of her life.
But faith cannot depend on purely temporal blessings and res-
cues.

As I talked about change being continual and the need for
successful ministers to counsel members because of it, one of my
informants shrugged and quipped, "Yes, everything's in a state
of continual change. It looks to me as if one-third of my con-

gregation is moving where it should be, one-third is doing the work, and one-third has probably outgrown me spiritually."

I laughed at his modest statement, for I doubted whether so many have outgrown him, but I understood. Men and women do not mature in lockstep, regardless of how you perceive Christianity, how forcefully you preach, and how well you counsel them. The people you counsel will be ambivalent about their rewards and responsibilities as Christians. So will you and I. To avoid becoming a legalistic Pharisee, we must remain in touch with our own feelings. It does little good to tell a troubled person to trust God and live in peace if we ourselves are frustrated and angry as we speak. Our nonverbal communication will betray us, and we do great harm if we are so filled with self-righteousness that we cannot accept the fact that we are less than perfect.

There are two major approaches to counseling that you will find useful: directive and non-directive.

Circumstances will often determine which of the two approaches should be used. As in the case of other things that a minister does on the job, the choice of directive or non-directive counseling will be a judgment call. Good judgment, your resources, the nature of the situation, and the character of the person involved will often determine which way to go.

Some time ago a pastor friend of mine was approached by the chairman of his board of trustees. He stated to Joel Wong that the sanctuary needed a new roof. Because the pastor had served the congregation from the beginning, the chairman wanted his opinions about the repair job. Joel told him:

We had nothing but trouble with the contractor who installed this roof initially. Couldn't meet our deadlines, tried to substitute cheaper materials, and used inexperienced labor for some of the work. It would be a major mistake to go back to him. On the other hand, the Donovan Company just completed reroofing the whole plant at Reformation Lutheran. Paul Nielsen and I belong to the Ministers' Association, and he was very pleased with the quality. Why don't you call them about a bid?

Reroofing the sanctuary is a big and expensive job, but a

simple and direct answer got the chairman started on it. The direct approach is not always so effective, however.

Directive Counseling

There often comes a time when emotions, ambitions, and differing views of life, worship, and spirituality will complicate directive counseling. You may then have to do some real research and deep thinking before giving a sound answer. I discovered this in a bitter experience with one of my students.

Brent Hanscomb was a big, handsome college senior who had majored in political science with a psychology minor. He intended entering politics after taking a degree in law but was tired of school and wanted to make some money for a few years. We met in my office and, as we talked, I almost casually stated that he might want to try for a commission in the military. I told him that the pay was pretty good, he would have a clothing allowance, and he would probably travel a good deal. The country was at peace at the time. Brent sat up in his chair, eyes bright, and told me he would do it. Would I, he asked, write a letter of recommendation for him? I did and he went to the Marine Corps. War came and he took his tank platoon into battle. Within a month or two a sniper shot Brent through his 163 IQ brain and he was gone—at least partly because I used a directive approach that I had no business using. I have been a lot less cavalier in applying *my* solutions to other persons' lives since then, and you should exercise the same restraint.

When you are in a situation where directive counseling is appropriate, use this method:

Relate to the person to create rapport.

Recognize circumstances as they see them.

Recommend appropriate choices and action.

Recover opportunities to recommend again.

When a person experiences a problem that seems to you to be solvable by directive counseling, begin by *relating* warmly and supportively. If you will make the effort to create rapport, other people will perceive you as trustworthy and helpful. When you

FIGURE 36 **Directive Counseling, Step 1**

relate warmly, you allow people to remain open and emotionally honest with you rather than concealing things that they fear would cause them pain. Begin by relating (figure 36).

Listen without rebuttal, criticism, interruption, or defense. Let the person speak to his or her heart's content without responding in an attempt to blame anyone or protect yourself or the church. When feedback seems appropriate, demonstrate your acceptance and sense of proportion through your verbal and nonverbal communication. The last thing you want is for the person to feel he must pay emotionally for coming to counsel with you. Some of the ideas outlined in the ACCEPT stage of the coaching process in chapter seven might help you achieve the needed rapport.

The next step to follow when using directive counseling is for you to *recognize* the problem as the person sees it. To better understand the situation, ask supportive questions and pay attention to the answers. Listen selectively so as to hear both what is being said and what is not. Act supportively toward the person and listen with emotional honesty. Remember that the goal of directive counseling is not to allocate blame or find a scapegoat but to help the person solve a specific problem and become a more responsible Christian and parish member.

If you ask supportive questions and listen to the answers, the person will normally indicate the best way for you to respond to his or her need. When given an opportunity to speak honestly and without worrying about self-protection, the other person will usually reach back into his or her unconscious knowledge to give *you* the answers needed to offer appropriate help. The process can then be diagrammed like figure 37.

Only after you have created or extended a good relationship by relating authentically to the other person and come to know what the problem is as he or she sees it, can you *recommend* a

FIGURE 37 **Directive Counseling, Step 2**

FIGURE 38 **Directive Counseling, Step 3**

solution that makes sense. It should go without saying that there will be times when you have to gather information from other sources. You cannot be expected to know everything about topics beyond your expertise. Use appropriate sources to gather information and only then recommend solutions that the other person understands. See figure 38.

Before asking the person to use the suggested solution or take your advice, encourage him to play the devil's advocate with you. Ask the person to use the potential-problem-analysis process to anticipate what could go wrong with your solution for his or her problem. (You may want to review chapter five for this.) Use the feedback from the PPA Process to *recover* opportunities to make your directive counseling even better. Directive counseling then looks like figure 39.

If you use this directive-counseling process, you will have been supportive by relating, will have been more concerned with solving a problem than finding a scapegoat, and will have kept the person involved and participating in the process. In addition, you will have taught the person to look at his needs in a new way, better equipped to do his best without bringing the matter to you in the future. Both your effectiveness and his confidence will be enhanced as he matures as a Christian worker.

Non-Directive Counseling

The most common approach to pastoral counseling, one that a Supporter uses automatically much of the time, is more complex. While directive counseling deals with decisions that are often obvious, non-directive counseling is needed for more complex concepts and choices. It is disastrous for a pastor to offer simple, direct solutions to complex problems. As H. L. Mencken of the old *Baltimore Sun* wrote, simple and neat solutions are

FIGURE 39 **Directive Counseling, Step 4**

appealing to many people who do not think, but they have the trait of being simple, neat—and wrong!

Even when a pastor's answer for a complex situation is "correct," giving a member an answer rather than helping him discover the solution personally does nothing to help him mature. No overall gain is achieved, and the person has to come in again when something goes wrong at a later time. The last thing a successful pastor wants to perpetuate is a dependency cycle in which the people of the parish fail to mature. Besides, what kind of simple and neat answers could you give to such questions as the following?

> I'm at my wit's end, Pastor. You recently preached a sermon in which you stated that as Christ is the Head of the church, so the husband is the head of the family. I want to believe that, but Jack has started drinking heavily again. I can't afford to clothe the girls now, have had to stop music lessons for them, and he has forbid me to bring them to church again. The worse thing is that he has started fondling the girls when he comes home drunk. When I try to stop him, he beats me with his fists. Tell me what to do. Shall I let him be the head of the family or shall I leave before he sexually abuses the girls? I have no family here in the state, and he's spent all our money on his drinking and womanizing. He has threatened to kill all of us if I tell anyone about this.

> John's company wants to transfer him to Albuquerque to manage the plant there. It would be a great promotion for him but a real problem for me. I'm halfway through my master's program in nursing and supervisor at Baptist Hospital in Loma Linda. How can I help him reach his goals without sacrificing my own? Is his manufacturing paint more important to God and humans than my teaching surgical nursing at the university? Tell me how to resolve this.

Almost every kind of lasting satisfaction is a by-product of having long-range reasons for life and fulfilling work. It is the men and women who worship sincerely, work loyally, love warmly, and play enthusiastically who find the greatest happiness in life. Fulfillment may come from a number of sources. You may find momentary pleasure from eating a candy bar, from making love, from listening to some great passage of music played well by a skilled musician. But, in themselves, such

pleasures cannot compare to a career that leaves some section of
the world a better place. They cannot hold a candle to a loving
relationship that has developed a fine patina of mutual joy from
years of shared spiritual values, positive attitudes, and responsible choices being invested in the beloved.

Non-directive counseling by a pastor should be used to help
people reach the best solutions for their lives without your dominating them in any way. An outsider simply does not have
enough facts to make as good a choice as the person in the
situation. Giving *advice* to men and women about their careers,
marriages, and families is too close to playing God.

There is another side to that coin. Making the congregation
happy with the individual seeking counseling is not a legitimate
goal of non-directive counseling either. We dare not confuse com-
pliance with Christian commitment or equate the seeking of
personal prestige in church governance with spirituality. Every
parish has some who march to another drum than middle-class,
Anglo-Saxon mores, ambitions, and customs. Such people often
see the role of the church in a different light than the typical
member, and they are often thought of as disruptive when they
call for the congregation to consider problems that do not personally affect the majority. To try to blend the parish membership into a single world-view that offends no one is a fast trip
to being neither hot nor cold. And you know what the Scriptures
say about that!

To be effective as any kind of counselor, be as emotionally
honest as you can. If I am angry about something, trying to find
my way through a personal challenge, or preoccupied with anything but the relationship with the counselee, I will not go
through with the session. When distracted by my own feelings, I
have found that I send too many conflicting messages. I cannot
be authentic or congruent, and that confuses the persons seeking counsel. It sometimes happens, when I tell them why my
mind is not on their problems, that I find relief and am able to
shift over to my role as counselor. That happened not too long
ago.

Nell had come in to see me, and I was preoccupied because my
daughter-in-law was in extended labor with her third child.
Now, I'm an old pro at this! Not just counseling but grandfather-
ing—it was my fifth—but I couldn't get past my concern. I told

Nell that I was preoccupied and somewhat anxious for several reasons. She suggested that we could reschedule. When we did, she began telling me about the birth of her children. She hesitated for a moment as a look of frustration crossed her face. She told me that her husband had never been able to accept the fact that both children were girls and there was no male heir to carry on the family name. She had some health problems and could have no more children, and he had never forgiven her. I interrupted at that point and asked whether the husband realized that *he* set the gender of the child at conception. She quipped that while he was bright, he wasn't all that understanding about the girls. By that time I was hooked, and we went on to have a very productive session. We had a good session because I was emotionally honest with Nell. I accepted the fact that my own mind is not a computer, that I have things that are more important to me than my livelihood, and I shared those feelings. Our relationship remained strong because I was authentic, and I gained relief by being emotionally honest.

I exposed you to the ASRAC method in the previous chapter, and I recommend that you also use it for non-directive counseling. Here it is again:

Accept the client's feelings and statements without contradiction, defense, or interpretation. Remain authentic and allow him or her to gain catharsis by speaking as frankly and frequently as necessary.

Share the client's emotions, statements, and fears by agreeing as much with him or her as you authentically or congruently can. Say such things as: "I understand that. If it had happened to me, I'd feel much the same way." "I hate it when people abuse me, so I can feel for you." "Why don't you tell me more about your happiness when the baby came."

Reflect the client's emotions as best you understand them, to demonstrate your understanding. You do this best by paraphrasing what he or she said. Preface the paraphrase with something like: "Let me see if I understand you. May I do that?"

Pause here to shift gears from dealing with his or her feelings about the situation to the facts of dealing with it in a mature manner. Then go on to the next two steps:

Add new information so the client can see the situation more completely. Since men and women normally want to be logical, they will cooperate and think things through better when new information is added. Preface the new facts with this statement: "Think about this and see if it doesn't make sense." You will be surprised how often they will say it does and move toward an informed choice.

Confirm the client's choice by asking for an agreement. Get the person to close the issue on a positive note that both of you can remember and rely on. Don't make the mistake of dealing with facts first and then discovering later that deep-seated feelings continue to boil over to throw all the facts and logic aside.

In my leadership seminars I suggest that each participant plug into this process by creating a number of situations or imagining some from the past. Plan how you could, or should have, used the *Accepting, Sharing,* and *Reflecting* steps, and then wait before planning how to use the *Adding* and *Confirming* steps. Think through ways to use this counseling approach with the people of your parish.

The Fourfold Nature of Pastoral Leadership

The preceding four chapters have shown how to come full circle in leadership by borrowing from the strengths of each personality pattern. You may have started by solving problems, as a good Comprehender does automatically, and then gone on to decision making, using the natural skills of a Controller. In other situations, you must shift from dealing primarily with facts and objectives to a greater concern for feelings. You have learned to be an Entertainer, how to coach rather than criticize. Finally, you moved ahead to counsel directively and non-directively, like an effective Supporter. Flexibility is of an essence, since—depending on your own personal pattern—some of these skills may seem awkward at first. All can be developed with time and practice by using the processes outlined. Each approach is important to your success as a logical, objective, inspirational, and supportive pastoral leader and to the ongoing fellowship and Christian maturity of your congregation.

PART 3

Managing Relationships Wisely

9

Basic Principle of Interpersonal Relationships

There is a basic principle of interpersonal relationships that every dedicated minister should learn as early as possible in his or her career. It is a principle that must be communicated to the people of the parish in many different ways. This other side of the leadership coin focuses on the sound understanding of human relationships as the best way to lead a successful congregation.

> . . . we should all please our brothers for their own good, in order to build them up in the faith.
>
> Romans 15:2

A recent study conducted with more than a thousand pastors in a major denomination revealed that their major concern was learning better ways to manage interpersonal relationships. I did not conduct the research, but it certainly confirms my own work and my experiences in dealing with pastors in the English-speaking world. The basic principle of better interpersonal relationships is this:

Good things happen to people who cooperate.

I am not so naive as to think that good things have always occurred in the lives of men and women who give their best to

God and church. That would eliminate the apostle Paul, many of the prophets, several disciples, and even Jesus himself—to say nothing of the martyrs for Christ down through the ages and the men and women of faith and devotion who are caught up in the massive economic disruptions of our era. Some slippery and malicious characters enter different congregations for their own reasons that have little to do with spiritual worship and growth.

Although I admit writing a book called *Nice Guys Finish First* that was translated and became a best-seller in several nations, I never wrote a line saying that "naive guys and gals finish first." It appears that when some people hear me talking about nice people doing well in life or quoting the basic principle they grow disturbed and angry. Some say it just isn't so in the real world. In New Zealand recently, one woman snorted loudly enough to be heard all through a large meeting room and said that was the craziest thing she had ever heard.

Even more challenging was my experience with a talk-show host in one of the larger television stations in Detroit, Michigan. I was told I would have six minutes to promote my book and to tell what it was all about. When I arrived on camera, the host, a fellow named John Kelley, sat me on a stool before the people, held a copy of *Nice Guys Finish First* to the camera, and loudly announced that this was the most absurd thing he had ever seen. There was no way, he stated loudly, that a nice person could make it successfully in this lousy, rotten world.

He then turned to his live audience and asked how many of them agreed with this dunce on the stool (his body language sent the message loud and clear). About half the audience raised their hands to show they wanted to believe that nice people could make it. He then asked how many agreed with him that nice people would be steamrollered by life. The remaining half raised their hands to endorse that host's view that a nice guy or gal had no chance in the world of succeeding.

John then turned toward me, motioned for the cameras to zoom in to see me sweat in discomfort, and said, "Now *Doctor* DeVille, how are you going to handle that?" He was very sarcastic, but I was ready. "It all depends on how you define nice guy or gal," I replied. "If you think of a nice person as a marshmallow, a doormat, or a wimp, I have to agree with you. That kind of nice guy doesn't have much of a chance. I have never advised anyone to face life from such an attitude. But, if you define nice guys and gals as I do, it's an entirely different matter." I explained that I see a nice person as one who works from the following triad:

Manages interpersonal relationships very well

Shares the rewards of cooperation with others

Creates a community of continual achievers

John sat stunned as the cameras swung back and forth, panning from me to him, to the audience and back to me for thirty seconds or more. That's an eternity of dead air on a talk show, but he sat silent while I crossed my arms and leaned back on my stool, having spoken my piece. He finally stood and gradually took charge of the program once more. He said aloud and on camera, "Well, I'll be damned! I had never thought of it that way." When he finally came fully out of his reverie, he turned to the live audience and asked for a show of hands again. "Under these conditions," he asked, "how many of you still disagree with the learned doctor?" Only two people raised their hands this second time. I had won them over. The next Sunday I contacted my pastor, told him the story, and suggested that with *my* conversion rate we would have the largest congregation in the world! John had given me a full twenty-five minutes on the show rather than the intended six!

I understand that naive people often get hurt by the users and abusers of society, but any pastor can use my basic principle to win the consistent commitment of the people in a parish. This is your promise—not that you can control acts of nature and God—that you will do your best as their leader in doing three things. You will manage interpersonal relationships well, will share the rewards of dedication, and will create a community of believing achievers in which the members support each other. This should be your spiritual contract with your congregation.

A realistic pastor does not pretend to be perfect or to have control over all the important events of parish and personal life. You can promise, however, with all your strength and wisdom to give people *good for good*. You can promise to reward people physically, psychologically, and philosophically in body, mind, and spirit. You can promise to the best of your finite human nature that they will get full credit for everything they do, that you will not burden them with busy work, and that you will do your utmost to help them mature in the Christian life. There is every reason in this world and in the hereafter to make this commitment to your people. Good things happen to people who help make your parish a better congregation.

There is another element in the basic principle, however:

Bad things don't happen to people who cooperate.

Once more, you are not God. Accidents occur, and deeply loved children develop leukemia. We all experience what Viktor Frankl calls the "tragic triad" of suffering, guilt, and death. That is part of the human condition, and all you will be able to do is teach your people how to use each tragedy and setback as a stepping-stone to greater maturity. But, to the best of your ability as pastor and friend, you will not humiliate or allow to be devalued by others the people who take you at your word.

Like a good army officer who sees that his soldiers are fed and sheltered before meeting his own needs, so a pastor sees to the satisfactions of the people. By doing this, any leader is secure in the knowledge that his or her own satisfaction will be all the greater later on, as more and more people respond to better use of interpersonal trade-offs. You will not blame people for failures beyond their control, despite how much relief you gain by expressing your frustration. You will not hide when people need you but will work productively until circumstances return to normal. You will give credit when it is due, thus transmuting mutual respect, creativity, and performance into the pure gold of an achieving community of Christians.

Finally, this aspect of the Basic Principle must be used cautiously:

Good things don't happen to people who don't cooperate.

That statement sounds cruel, but I believe it is valid according to the Epistles of Paul and the teachings of Jesus. Because you are finite and there are only so many things you can do in a day, you cannot afford to give too much of your time to people and situations when there is no cooperative response. When I was a young minister, I inherited a congregation thickly interspersed with deadwood. Worse, it was in a denomination that worked from a connectional system in which we had to pay our budgets according to the number on the rolls.

I set up a calling program to reach every member who was not attending services fairly regularly or had not contributed financially to the church over the past few years. We were fair about it, sending letters and making phone calls, but for those remaining on the rolls without having moved to another community, I finally went to see them. I suggested that since the congregation was apparently no longer meeting their needs and no longer important to them, they should resign. Then we who were paying the bills would not have to carry them at the state level financially, would not have to supply services when their children were getting married, or see to their burial when they died.

Some people grew angry with me, but I remained firm and fair. If the congregation was still important enough for them to remain on the rolls, I asked them to give us some tangible support with their work, money, and worship. If not, I suggested that they find a church in which they could feel comfortable and do the work of God there. Of course, I am not talking about the homebound elderly or infirm in any form, or even the men and women who are trying to work their way through serious intellectual doubts. Great patience must be exercised with the latter, but with some you must say that the congregation is a community in which all capable members are expected to give to God and humankind in a variety of ways.

No pastor or church should be expected to support and continually cope with those men and women who actively or indirectly frustrate the activities and programs being implemented. There will be times when you must say, "Good things don't happen here to people who don't cooperate with us."

The basic principle of interpersonal relationships is effective for one major reason. People want the *quid pro quo* that will be discussed in greater detail in the following chapter. We all prefer *pleasure to pain* in the physical aspects of life, *Power/prestige to devaluation* in the psychological area, and *Purpose/permanence to meaninglessness* in the spiritual area.

People all want to be useful in their relationships. When you use your skills, authority, and power to help them gain pleasure, prestige/power, and purpose/permanence in their relations with others and with God, they will give you their consistent cooperation. Teach your people in as many ways as possible that *good things happen to people who cooperate in this community of believers and achievers.*

10

The Principle of Psychological Reciprocity

This principle of interpersonal relationships sounds simple on the surface, but it is actually rather profound in application. A child can understand it but entire nations and civilizations have collapsed because their leaders abused the concept. Jesus spoke about it long before I did:

"Do for others just what you want them to do for you."
Luke 6:31

Not only Jesus but an entire assortment of later-day psychologists state that in normal relationships and settings, men and women consistently react to others as they are first treated. This means that unless a person has a hidden agenda or ulterior motives, you can set the stage for him or her to mature, to help in the work of the church, and to deal in a better, more responsible way with you. We all take our behavioral and attitudinal cues as a means of interacting appropriately. How we treat others is normally the way they treat us. I know no one who demonstrated this more clearly than Michael Withers from Liverpool, England. The young Briton had come to the United States to do his doctorate in psychology at the University of Chicago. Once in the city of Sandberg—with its brawny shoulders, unique governmental institutions, and millions of people—Michael was fascinated and tried to learn everything about everything. He poked and peered into all kinds of activities, made friends with many different people, and generally had the time of his life. Some of his professors and the other students told him repeatedly that he was going to get into trouble because the neighborhood in which the university was situated had gone downhill. It was almost a slum, and he had better be careful of the people there. He ignored the warning in his enthusiasm.

Mike finally did get into trouble. One night he remained late in the library, started to his apartment when it closed, and saw a disturbance of some kind. He went over for a better look and was surrounded by half a dozen youth-gang members. They drew knives and demanded his money.

The young Englishman had never heard the term "psychological reciprocity," but he used the principle perfectly. He looked at the young men and said: "I most certainly will *not* give you my money, for I'm a guest in your country and don't think you should treat me so."

It got very quiet at that, as the youngsters digested the entirely unexpected information. Before anyone could react, however, Mike went on, "I would like to go to a pub with you and buy a round of ale and see if we could become friends."

The gang leader quietly closed his knife and looked embarrassed. He stated that he did know of a tavern that was open and allowed that he could go for a drink. After all, what is a gentleman to do when another gentleman asks him to have an ale with him? They went to the tavern, talked for hours until the business closed, and then the gang escorted Mike to his apartment—so that, as the leader said, "You won't get into any trouble. This is a rough neighborhood."

The story does not end there, however. From what he learned about the Principle of Psychological Reciprocity—that people normally react as they are treated—Mike did his doctoral dissertation on the relationships of inner-city gang members. He also set up a program through which fully half of the gang members received training to do jobs in the city that pulled them from their criminal lifestyle.

Reciprocity and Leadership

History, sacred and secular, is filled with leaders who learned to win the commitment and cooperation of large numbers of men and women by using interpersonal relationships wisely. Napoleon Bonaparte treated his soldiers so fairly that it is said that each private carried a marshal's baton in his knapsack in case he should be promoted in the field. The emperor demanded excellence, but he had learned that dedication must be earned if one's followers are to commit themselves to a cause.

John Wesley, founder and organizing genius of the Methodist Church, gathered a loyal group around him because he was first loyal to them. He gave of himself, and although his standards were high—including the *methodical* utilization of the means of grace that gave the group its eventual name—the people who did the work served well because they knew they were treated as he would have wanted for himself.

According to this principle of interpersonal interaction, whenever you, as leader, offer people trust, you will normally be trusted by your followers. If you offer esteem to men and women, they will come to respect you. If you become angry and manipulate others, they will become your adversaries. If you develop a leadership approach that enables people to achieve consistently, they will give you the extra support that will set you head and shoulders above your less-perceptive peers. What you plant in the congregation and nourish and water wisely through sound leadership is what you will reap.

You can multiply your effectiveness and efficiency in the parish by teaching your people to use this principle with each other. Remember, I wrote that I've never believed that naive people will succeed in their activities. Therefore, you must remain wise in the application of this interpersonal principle. If a neurotic member is determined to meet his or her abnormal needs by controlling the church's decisions, money, and activities, a smile and a cheery greeting will not save your career—any more than you can throw yourself on the mercy of the IRS if you goofed on your tax return! You will either have to develop ways to neutralize such a troublemaker or surrender the leadership of the parish. But even with such people you can use the principle to make life better for yourself and the others in the congregation.

A few years ago I taught classes about more effectively managing interpersonal relationships to the people who run the mountain ski program at Vail, Colorado. I taught for two days and then had the third day free to ski or do as I pleased. On my first day off, one of my students, an independent ski instructor named Tony Antonelli, saw me in a restaurant. He was excited about the concept of reciprocity. He said:

> This stuff *really* works. I'm an independent instructor, so I choose my own students and work my own hours. This morning I took a group of beginners out for a lesson and a hot-shot oil millionaire from Houston gave me some trouble. He started by putting on a lot of airs since he didn't realize he was on my turf rather than his. He said *"Boy,* pick up my skis and carry them for me!" In the past I would have insulted him in short order. Today, however, I recalled your concept of reciprocity and said—very politely—"John, on the mountain each person has the responsibility for his own equipment. It's too dangerous otherwise. Will the group please follow me to the lift?"

Tony laughed and told me how John picked up his skis and trotted after the group like a lamb. He concluded: "Not only did I feel better than if I had blasted him, so did the class. And I kept the guy for a student. He's coming back for a private lesson tomorrow. Your Principle of Psychological Reciprocity sure works."

Of course it does, for normal men and women want to get along with others, avoid conflict, and win respect and esteem. We will all defend ourselves when attacked, reacting to threats with either the flight-or-fight or the conceal-or-reveal syndromes, especially if someone is trying to get away with all the rewards of cooperation. But, from childhood on, we all develop a sense of equity about life and our place in it. We all want some kind of *quid pro quo* for our efforts.

Reciprocity in Action

To test the idea of reciprocity at a practical level, try the DeVille Sidewalk Test. Walk down the street in your city and smile at the first ten people you meet. Do not speak and do not slow down and look as if you were going to hold them up for money. Simply smile and keep walking. The vast majority of men and women will smile in return, nod, or even wish you a good day. The approach works in New Orleans, Auckland, Singapore, and even New York.

I was on a talk show in Manhattan one morning and the woman host challenged the reliability of the Sidewalk Test for New York. She doubted on the air that it would work in that high-pressure community where, according to her, people ignored each other. In rebuttal, I invited her to lunch at a nearby restaurant and won her over on the way. I put into practice what I had told the listeners and, to her surprise, got nine out of ten smiles with the first ten people we met.

On the next block, when conducting the Sidewalk Test, catch the eyes of the oncoming people and frown at them. Do it carefully, however. I have had people stop in their tracks and frown in return, shake their fists at me, even jump between parked cars to get away from me. I don't really expect you to try the Sidewalk Test—only slightly nutty psychologists actually do such things—but in each case the person responding was hooking into my mood, attitude, and behavior. As Jesus implied, it is the way humans are built, and you can use it in two different ways.

You can persuade people to do what is best for themselves and for the congregation by applying this principle. You can also recognize this tendency within yourself and refuse to let angry or unhappy people hook you into reacting as they are doing. You can use your knowledge and wisdom to remain a true leader rather than reacting in kind, as others do automatically and often destructively. Good leaders teach people not only how to follow but to lead when it is appropriate, for a congregation often has shifting relationships. In a volunteer group, a man or woman may lead some activities and be led in others. This will also occur for you. There will be times, say in a calling campaign or a financial drive, when you will be one of the foot troops while a banker or corporate executive in the congregation is running that part of the program. The following day, in a meeting of the congregation, you may well be presenting a plan for a new multi-million-dollar sanctuary.

A major portion of your responsibility is to create a congregational climate in which the members become mature and more and more responsible for themselves. Any psychological climate is made up of values, attitudes, expectations, beliefs, and choices. While atmospheric weather may change frequently according to meteorological circumstances, the general climate remains constant in a region. Storms occur in Hawaii and in

Tahiti, but the climate remains favorable for decades at a time. So it is within the church or any long-lived organization. Storms occur—especially when changes force people from their comfort zones—but the sound spiritual climate in a parish can go on for generations when the group is effectively challenged to serve God and the community and taught how to mature as Christians.

The Principle of Psychological Reciprocity is actually a binding psychospiritual contract between a leader and his or her followers, when applied wisely and well. All successful organizations, nations, and civilizations survive because of a finely balanced, time-proven system of sharing responsibilities and rewards. In our day, many of the traditional methods used by the church are no longer effective. One of the greatest challenges is the way that men and women today question the right of their organizations to manage their attitudes and acts. Members of Western-world corporations, universities, governmental units, and churches rarely believe that their leaders have any right to make decisions for them without their permission. As I said about my friend—who pointed to his clerical collar and growled, "Do it because I wear this and *you* don't!"—people reject power as such but still respond positively to leadership that persuades and influences. It is when leading in this manner that reciprocity becomes most effective.

Building Member Responsibility

The spiritual attitudes, positive attitudes, and high expectations you integrate in your interpersonal relationships not only create the reactions you want from others; their use will also help people mature as congregational leaders in their own right. There are few things a parish needs more than a large number of people who are ready and able to do well the things that must be accomplished.

Oddly enough, reciprocity gives a clue that the best way to persuade the members to take leadership responsibility is to give them the freedom to fail. It is only as we press to the limits, risking much for God but remaining enthusiastic about what we can accomplish, that great churches are built. You cannot get people to take chances, however, if they discover that they will be humilitated for their mistakes. Every person has to go through a learning curve before doing anything well, and work in the parish is no exception. By protecting the egos of men and women who are willing to risk failure, you can use reciprocity to show everyone else how to mature in service and most likely gain their loyal support when you stumble occasionally in your leadership capacity.

If the climate of a congregation is such that it requires an illustration of perfection or certitude before attempting new activities, it has been frozen into past decisions and assumptions. This is fatal, of course, because contemporary problems do not yield to yesterday's solutions. For example, in the early years of the twentieth century, the church tried to deal with the problem of widespread alcoholism by establishing national prohibition. The great experiment failed, and few people in today's church seriously expect to end the tragedy of alcoholism by the use of prohibition. Treatment is required, not an all-encompassing taboo.

Another area in which past solutions for contemporary problems can no longer work is divorce. I grew up in a denomination that would not only reject newcomers who were divorced but would discard long-standing members who experienced a marriage failure. I am in a different denomination now, but I suspect that should my old church do that today, they would have to close most meeting-houses!

People who have experienced failure in their lives and activities need to be reclaimed in every way and put to work in places where they can rebuild their sense of purpose and permanence in fellowship with God and the church. I know of no better way of doing this than by applying the Principle of Psychological Reciprocity, utilizing people to their limits and supporting them should they fail. Rather than criticize their efforts, use the correction-coaching process discussed in chapter seven.

The way that you deal with other people sets the stage for the way they will respond to you. Jesus said it first, and it's still sound human psychology for a pastoral leader to follow.

11

The Principle of
Selective Perception

Lt is a rule of thumb among Federal Aviation Administration employees who are investigating aircraft crashes to view eyewitness testimony with considerable skepticism. In many cases, the events as remembered by the witnesses are contradicted by the physical evidence. For example, a witness may insist that he or she heard the engine stop in mid-air and saw the aircraft fall because it had no power to sustain flight. Yet an investigation of the propeller will reveal that it is not bent back, as would have occurred were it standing still when it hit, but twisted sideways and gouged deeply, proving that it was still turning under engine power. The witness perceived it all wrong.

No experienced accident investigator believes that the witnesses are trying to deceive him, of course. Most know the principle I will discuss in this chapter—that we all see what we expect to see because we have the well-developed mind power to shape reality to fit our own preconceived notions. This happened at Pentecost, too.

> When they heard this noise, a large crowd gathered. They were all excited, because each one of them heard the believers talking in his own language. . . . But others made fun of the believers, saying, "These people are drunk!"
>
> Acts 2:6, 13

169

Emotional Screening

Because we humans seem to fear an intellectual or an emotional vacuum, we fill each void in our emotions or reasoning, even if we have to manufacture the filler out of ignorant conclusions, half-truths, or outright lies. At Pentecost, some of the crowd had a ready answer for those trying to understand the excitement, although their explanation was simple, neat, and wrong. We can state this as a generalization:

Men and women in leadership positions in the church, like everyone else, always filter all incoming information through a psychospiritual screen to keep from being confused or devalued by new information or relationships.

We all use this emotional screening process for several reasons. In the first place, the elimination of ideas and facts that would trouble us allows us to feel better about ourselves. We can protect our egos by rationalizing our mistakes in a number of ways. After a severe social blunder, we can run the experience through our self-protective screen and decide that the *faux pas* was not that bad or was justified. We can also convince ourselves that other people do much more serious things, so we are really all right in comparison. It is not healthy to continue browbeating and berating ourselves for past mistakes. We should learn how to forgive ourselves in light of Christ's acceptance of us, as long as we go on trying to do better the next time around.

In the second place, the use of a perceptual screen in our relationships allows us to better understand what is going on around us. It has a survival/success element to it. For example, imagine that you are at a meeting and quietly immersed in the drone of voices. You are paying little or no attention to the people around you and then, like a bolt out of the blue, you hear your name spoken across the room. You are immediately alert and discover that you not only heard your name but became aware that you also heard the sentence that preceded it! Your brain/ mind may have been idling in neutral, but something important (your name) automatically put it into gear.

As you manage interpersonal relationships more and more

successfully as a congregational leader, you will recognize the fact that everyone else does just what you do. Perfectly normal, self-centered men and women interpret all their activities and relationships according to the world-view or mind-set they have created for themselves while growing up. According to my $P = f(H \times E \times C)$ equation, we know what we know and generally refuse to yield to new facts that contradict our "knowledge" or emotions. What does this mean to you in your work?

As you interpret every conversation, action, and relationship to suit your satisfaction and best interest, so will every other person in the congregation see the choices and decisions to his or her advantage.

It is difficult to imagine a setting more conducive to misunderstandings, conflicts, and resentment than the unstructured, volunteer relationships encountered in a parish ministry. A leader has no control over people except that which they permit. As you deal with life-and-death issues in the present and in the hereafter, you get into the difficult situation of interpreting Scripture. How can you understand and meet the needs of hundreds of people with as many perceptual screens actively functioning and keep them from feeling bad or from perceived harm? This is obviously a difficult challenge.

Of course, just as few people are aware that they have a personality pattern or a world-view, few people understand that they have a perceptual screen. To them, "truth" is spelled with a capital T. As the king in *The King and I* sings in his confusion, we humans are all too willing to ". . . prove what we do not know is so." However, even if no one else in the congregation recognizes that everyone works through a personal perceptual screen, their leader had better know it!

Last year I attended an ecumenical meeting with a lay delegate from a nearby parish of my own denomination. She has long been a good friend of mine, and we have worked in different community programs. I have always found Lil to be a congenial, cooperative colleague, so it surprised me, when we started our committee work, to find her cranky and contentious. She challenged several statements made by the chairman, a minister from another denomination. Lil made the entire meeting an

unpleasant experience for me, since she reversed her position
several times and greatly complicated the issues. It was so out of
character for her that when we went to lunch, I tried to discover
the cause of her frustration, which seemed focused on the chairman.

She did not want to talk about it, but I used several of the
psychological techniques that persuade reluctant people to discuss their emotions and found what was bothering her. In just a
few minutes she said: "You can't trust the ministers from that
denomination. I've never known one who could be relied on
when something is really important, and he's no different."

I was surprised at Lil's appraisal, for in my years of association with the committee chairman, I have known him to be
honest and fair in our dealings. He has pastored a spiritual,
growing congregation that works well without a great deal of
friction. It seemed to me that Lil was reacting in an entirely
inappropriate manner, so I pressed still further into her psyche.
An unfortunate story boiled out.

My friend had grown up in the other denomination, and when
she was in high school, the pastor she had trusted was caught
molesting little boys. The official church board tried to keep the
tragedy quiet, but a community newspaper reporter found out
about it and the entire congregation suffered greatly. Lil felt
betrayed and never forgot the incident. The experience wells up
every time she has to meet with a minister from that denomination. She measures all of them through the perceptual screen
that developed a serious bias when she was a girl, but I am sure
the denomination has no more emotionally disturbed ministers
than our own.

The Roots of Bigotry

In the not-too-distant past, a virtual army of white men and
women conspired to keep black people out of the nation's schools,
businesses, hospitals, and churches. They used every cliché—
from the curse of Cain, through Darwin, and on to Jensen—to
convince one another that black people could not think well
enough to serve effectively when mental effort was required. I
have sat in meetings where business owners and managers
stated that they would never hire black employees because they

would not work hard enough to carry their part of the load. Yet those men and women had seen, as has everyone of my generation, black people working harder than anyone else in our society—for hours at a time, with sweat pouring from their bodies and at low wages. The perceptual screens of such bigots filter from consciousness any and all facts that would contradict their biased "knowledge" about blacks.

Interestingly enough, one of the most outspoken critics of our attempts to bring black people into mainstream American life confirmed my view of his perceptual screen. He told me he would not hire Japanese-American workers either, because they worked so fast and hard that they discouraged the white workers. He was saying that he did not want to examine his mind-set, because doing so would force him to revise the self-protective mechanisms developed in his youth. If he did, he would no longer be able to exclude automatically any person and any concept that would force him from his comfort zone. This was all self-serving, although he hid that from himself by using "facts" to explain his rigid views. Don't *you* do the same, even though a large percentage of the church in America is the last bastion of institutionalized racism. In some parts of the United States, not one church in two hundred will admit black worshipers!

Recognizing Mind-Sets

There is a subtle trap for ministers who do not understand how their own perceptual screens work. It is what Bonaparte called "making a picture" in the mind of a battle commander. He continually warned his generals against using past, isolated experiences to distort the reality of their present battles. He had learned that rigid leaders who could not adapt to new facts would get a lot of good men killed needlessly.

In the novel *The Silver Lady* by James Facos, a character drawn from the author's battle-flying experience in World War II told his Quaker friend that life was the greatest trap of all. Hagan had grown up with a brutal father and a terrified mother. Each attempt he made to escape to a more fulfilling life came to little because his negative world-view led him to sabotage his relationships with people around him. Finally Hagan joined the Army Air Force to train as a gunner in a B-17. When the young man reached England to fly combat missions over Europe, he found himself in the ultimate trap. Only about one man out of ten escaped being killed, shot down, captured, or maimed. Hagan was even more cynical, bitter, and unreliable than before, because his mind-set was that life was not worth living.

It took the self-sacrificial death of his only friend, Tom the Quaker boy, to teach Hagan that the crew was greater than the sum of its parts. Tom was a Christ-like figure who showed Hagan that by mutual love and trust they might beat the odds, although individuals might be lost in the effort. Few men ever know such companionship and support. A true friend's death in the ball turret changed Hagan's mind-set, and he escaped the mental trap.

A minister who has an understanding perceptual screen that enables him or her to support and to love the members deeply sets the stage for people to mature in commitment to Christ and the church. It is far better to allow human flaws and short-comings to pass harmlessly through your screen from time to time than to challenge everyone who does not meet your expectations. Most of us blunder along with a mixture of wisdom and foolishness, either rising to heights of compassion or wallowing in the mud of selfishness so that our commitment falters. As I understand Christianity, being in Christ does not make us perfect, but it does grant us forgiveness. That is why we need Christ as Advocate. When we see the sham of pretense for what it is, we need not demand that others meet goals we do not set for ourselves.

A very wise man demonstrated this principle to me. When I was a youngster, I saw that some people had taken advantage of him. He had treated them kindly, and they betrayed his trust. Still later it happened again. I expressed my frustration and told him that he should tighten up his activity so it would not cost him anything personally.

He changed not a thing but shrugged and explained that he would rather be taken advantage of every second Tuesday for the rest of his life than become so cynical and suspicious that no one could ever steal anything from him again. There were no locks on his barns, no time cards, and no penalties exacted. I realized that 99 percent of the people who came into contact with him followed the Principle of Psychological Reciprocity to give him what he offered them. He was not as naive as I first thought, but a very good human who made others feel good about themselves when working with him.

To avoid the complications that can arise because men and women interpret activities and relationships according to their personal perceptual screens, have people write down their interpretations and understandings when they are critical. This may require a little more time but not nearly so much time as having to meet over and over to fight brush fires that need never have started in the first place. As a parish leader, try especially hard to lay aside your own mind-set in order to understand what the members are doing and thinking. Don't let a lot of emotional baggage complicate your leadership.

In the last analysis, especially when serious issues are before you, remember that each person in the situation will understand and interpret what is happening and what is decided in such a way that it meets his or her own views. All people interpret life according to a world view that makes sense to them and will therefore accept ideas that confirm their needs and reject those that do not. Since this is done unconsciously and automatically, make sure you have real agreement before pressing people to accept your views and plans for the congregation. Understanding mind-sets can avoid a great deal of dissatisfaction and conflict later.

12

The Principle of Logical Justification

In the last book of J.R.R. Tolkien's fantasy trilogy, *Lord of the Rings*, Gimli the dwarf and Legolas the elf are waiting for the men in their company to make up their minds about taking a particular course of action. Gimli complains that it is as plain as a pikestaff what must be done and that humans take an inordinate amount of speech among themselves to reach a decision. Legolas shrugs, agrees with him, and implies that such is the way of men and that they might as well get used to it if they are to remain in the company.

So it is with humans. Men and women need a great deal of discussion when working in groups in order to make sure that everyone knows what to do. Equally important is the fact that we need to examine activities and choices and relationships in order to convince ourselves that our decisions are based on logical premises. To us of the industrial world, basing decisions on emotions rather than on objective data is somehow considered inferior.

I understand that it is dangerous to sail a ship from the harbor against the tide or to take an aircraft off a runway with the wind at your back. Those considerations involve technical facts, however, and not the emotional reasons that impel people to build great ships and flying machines in the first place. Every outstanding activity, choice, or decision starts as an image in someone's mind—an emotionally conceived dream of what can be done. Thus we read in Scripture:

177

That night Paul had a vision in which he saw a Macedonian standing and begging him, "Come over to Macedonia and help us!"

Acts 16:9

My interpretation of the Principle of Logical Justification is this:

We very often make our most important decisions based on our emotions and then search to find logical-appearing reasons to justify our activities, attitudes and relationships.

Everyone who has impulsively fallen in love with a stranger has done this. "Love at first sight" is always based on emotions rather than on facts, as is our attraction to a company, a college, or a congregation.

In the churches we have known, Roberta and I have worked as a pastoral couple and then as lay workers after I entered college teaching and writing. Since our relationship with Christ is strong and the place of the church in our affiliations is very high, when we moved to Minneapolis we decided to use a calm-and-collected approach to choosing a parish in which to work and worship. We got a map and located five or six churches of our denomination within easy driving distance. We agreed that we would visit each one, starting with the closest, make a list of all the good and bad points, and reach a logical choice. The plan sounded great.

On the first Sunday morning, we got the kids ready and drove a few blocks to the nearest congregation. It was summer and many of the members were away, so I am not sure how it all happened. Before we got away, Roberta had been drafted into the choir and I had helped the associate minister serve communion. Before we got a chance to visit the second congregation, she was committed to singing a solo and I was chairing a committee. That was fifteen years ago, and we have yet to evaluate those five other congregations! We all work from our emotions first and foremost in almost all of our relationships and choices.

For decades the psychologists of Madison Avenue advertising firms have used subliminal persuasion techniques to tap the streams of emotions that flow through the human unconscious. The automobile industry builds sports cars, often at a loss, to intensify traffic in showrooms where dealers want to sell their family sedans. One well-known baking company prints the word *sex* in tiny type on their crackers to persuade people to buy them. Several liquor companies have their advertising artists work almost-invisible grotesque figures with death heads into the ice cubes of the highballs pictured in magazines. Professor Wilson Key writes about this in great detail in his book *Subliminal Seduction*. It is Key's contention that such advertisements appeal to the hidden death wish held by abusers of alcohol and other drugs.

Emotions and Cultural Traditions

For aeons before the development of writing and mathematics, our ancestors survived as clans and villages by transmitting crucial information to succeeding generations through oral traditions. In a preliterate society, there was no other way to make sure the children learned what they and the clan needed to survive. Each tribe needed every possible member to till the soil, scrape the hides, herd the flocks, fish the rivers, and fight off raiding warriors. It was in this manner that a tradition developed that birth control was evil: it decreased the people's chances of surviving as a clan. With swineherds infected with trichinosis, a tradition developed that pork, which remained dangerous after being cooked briefly over a puny twig or dung fire, was not fit for human consumption. In lands where water was too scarce to be used for washing and bathing, people cleaned themselves after bowel movements with the left hand and dipped the right into the communal meal. This custom helped prevent the spread of disease.

For ages, people everywhere accepted their own traditions—until philosophers and theologians eventually "justified" the rules with religious concepts that had nothing to do with the original reasons. There had to be some logical explanation for each tradition, and some inventive mind found it and internalized it in the clan's religious practices, thus preventing any dangerous experimentation.

In the case of birth control, dusty Hindu peasants, men and

women from fever-infested swamps of Africa, and residents of
Back Bay Boston mansions suffer alike from sexual frustration
and create horrendous population problems because of the emotions still caused by now-useless traditions. As time passes and
civilization changes, some traditions not only become useless;
they become harmful.

Consider the rejection of pork by millions of Muslims and
Jews around the world. The initial refusal to eat pork was a wise
one to follow in earlier times. It was, however, internalized as
part of their religious beliefs and frozen forever in their
cultures. Or, if not forever, at least long enough to cause major
nutrition problems for the poor and needy of the world. Every
major nation of the Northern Hemisphere, (except for the
United States) has eradicated trichinosis from its swineherds.
With breeding stock from Denmark or Germany, a hardy and
inexpensive source of protein could be introduced to relieve hun-
ger in the crowded, poverty-stricken cities of the Islamic nations. This will not happen, of course, because the leaders and
their followers are still making many decisions on the basis of
their emotions rather than on facts and will continue to do so as
long as the human race survives.

Reinforcement Listening

What has all this to do with the parish pastor? A great deal! A
few months ago I was in a committee meeting in which we were
to decide the professional fate of a pastor. One of the members—a
Controller in personality as well as controller of finance in his
company—tried to head off my opposing point of view with this
statement: "Let's all agree in advance to deal only with facts
tonight. Emotions have no place in our decisions."

I could not restrain myself. I shot back, "Emotions have *everything* to do with it." I was right, of course, for within ten minutes
he was red to the gills, I was pawing the floor, the committee
chairman was acting shell-shocked, and the congregation's senior lay-leader had run out into the hall to keep from throttling
several of us. We finally worked it out, and my adversary and I
spent a pleasant morning together a short time ago, cooking
hundreds of feet of sausage for a pancake breakfast. The climate
of that congregation is good, although storms occur from time to

time, because we first act emotionally and then try to find ways to justify our choices.

If you find yourself in some difficulty because the tides of emotions are running high, search out the hidden fears and the secret agendas that are behind so many church disasters. Use the client-centered method that Carl Rogers describes in his books *Counseling and Psychotherapy* and *On Becoming a Person*. This allows you to shape the discussion in such a way that the person tells what you want to know and what you often *need* to know. You can elicit the information without being rude or demanding. The process is actually a form of "reinforcement listening."

Begin by getting the person alone, putting him or her at ease, and asking key questions. As the answers come, really listen. Search for cues that will help you understand, support, and reward the other person as he or she speaks. A good listener is rare in our take-charge, do-it-now civilization, so avoid the mistakes I see listeners make. In my book *The Psychology of Witnessing,* I suggested that a good listener will avoid the following:

Prejudging people by assuming answers in advance

Focusing on facts and ignoring feelings

Ignoring the real meanings of words used

Pretending to listen while planning rebuttal

Letting personal emotions block our feelings

Going off on tangents that destroy rapport

When listening for the crucial emotions that are hidden beneath the logical justification perceived on the surface, do this: *Respond to the concerns that are important to the discussion and remain uncommunicative about the things that are not.*

If you are trying to discover why a woman is opposed to the church's supporting a Cambodian family—saying it would be too expensive to take on while you are running a $400,000 annual budget—get her talking about the money and listen. Even if she talks about her daughter's wedding, listen according to the suggestions given above. *But do not respond,* as that would reinforce her discussion of things that are irrelevant to her opposition. Don't communicate verbally or nonverbally.

When she does speak about the financial state of the congregation, about families, about the kinds of things the church should be doing, reward her with a quiet statement like "I see," or "That's interesting," or "Tell me more." You can also use a smile or a nod when she moves the conversation where you want it to go. By responding positively to the ideas that are important to the issue at hand and relating warmly to maintain rapport, you can shape the conversation and help the other person recognize the elements he or she may have overlooked.

Many times in years past I have had to counsel people sent to me in lieu of going to jail. They always came with a great deal of resentment and fear, with no intention of telling anything that might get back to the judge or police. Yet, with the exception of a few people with psychopathic disorders, I have almost always been able to gain their trust and persuade them to talk about things they vowed not to tell me about a few minutes earlier.

The point to remember in using the client-centered approach is to use your skills legitimately and for spiritual purposes to dig beneath the surface blocks to the real reasons that stop participation. Even the most compulsive talker will eventually wind down so you can steer the conversation to productive areas.

As you do this, you indicate that you are trying to share the hurt, the anxieties, the confusion, and the misapprehensions of life. In the above example, as the woman speaks more and more authentically about her feelings regarding the refugee couple, wait until she reaches a crucial statement and use the paraphrase technique of the ASRAC process discussed in chapter seven. Say something like "Let me see if I understand you," or "Are you trying to tell me that you . . . ? or "Do you mean that you feel . . . ?"

By combining the two techniques and responding to statements that move the conversation in the way you need, information about her emotions will be uncovered. I can't begin to tell you how powerful this simple method is when used wisely to break through the reserve of a person using the Principle of Logical Justification. Try it. Before you realize it, certainly before the other person has time to think about it, the feelings will begin to be translated into verbal and nonverbal communication. This goes even beyond the ASRAC method by more specifically reinforcing the speaker at vital points. You can reach the juncture where you can say something like:

> Let me see if I understand you now. Are you telling me that you are worried that the other people in our community will think that we're bringing Communist sympathizers into town if we support the Cambodians? Is that what you are telling me?

If she agrees, you have reached a "discovery agreement" with her. You can go on:

"How would that affect us in the church here?" As she continues to speak, listen once more as you plan ways to defuse her fears, deal with the probable racism involved, and understand her use of money as an excuse.

To persuade her, you must not sound like a snake-oil salesman, of course, but continue to *relate* warmly, *recognize* her views as she sees them, *recommend* a way out of the situation and *recover* opportunities to deal with her again. (See chapter eight.) Reinforce her expression of emotions so she can remain authentic, or emotionally honest. Put her feelings into words as they emerge and ask for confirmation that you have it right. Work from the general to the more specific by reinforcing appropriate responses and ask her to accept your mutual "discovery" as a new explanation of why she should drop her opposition.

Had you accepted her surface explanation that her resistance to supporting a Cambodian family was financial, you could have argued yourself blue in the face and never come close to the hidden emotions. By listening and working from a client-centered approach, you have been able to get to her emotions and deal with them in a constructive manner. Better yet, she will probably leave with stronger feelings about you as a pastor.

13

The Principle of
Appropriate Rewards

Both experimental and clinical psychologists work from a premise that can be very valuable to pastors who are learning better ways of managing interpersonal relationships. The Principle of Appropriate Rewards is this:

All men and women, by themselves or in the company of others, make an attempt to continue the activities and relations that reward them and to avoid the situations that deprive them of desired rewards.

This sounds simple on the surface, but it is loaded with implications for men and women in leadership positions. You might assume that everyone who deals with other people knows from childhood that humans prefer a pat on the back to a sharp stick in the eye, but many obviously do not. Religious denominations, corporations, banks, colleges, political parties, and even nations have lost their way and collapsed because the leaders no longer shared the rewards of commitment with the rank-and-file members who were paying the bills and doing the work.

An athlete who runs in a race cannot win the prize unless he obeys the rules. The farmer who has done the hard work should have the first share in the harvest.

2 Timothy 2:5–6

185

We humans are seldom satisfied with what we have, do, and become. We remain restless, striving to expand our horizons and reach new goals in most situations. Therefore, we do not merely accept whatever payoffs life gives us through the luck of the draw; we actively seek rewards in the physical, psychological, and philosophical aspects of life.

The Search for Satisfaction

In her marvelous epic of the American Plains Indians, *Hanta Yo,* Ruth Bebee Hill demonstrates quite clearly this normal human seeking for satisfaction. She reveals, as have other historians who are not completely biased by their own experiences as white people, a beautiful way of life. The Plains Indians—the Dakota tribes, the Cheyenne, the Absaroka, and others—were perhaps the wealthiest men and women of all time. They followed the bison, which gave them natural resources beyond comprehension. One hundred thousand humans, hunting from horseback with powerful bows and lances, lived off thirty million animals that weighed in at a thousand pounds each.

Because the bison supplied almost all of their food, shelter, and clothes, and horses carried their burdens and provided transportation, virtually everyone was freed from most labor. The people had time to contemplate the meanings of life, the purposes of their existence, the relationships between one another. Among the many concepts they developed was an intricate rewards system that differed only slightly in each tribe or family of tribes. The men were warriors who went on raids, not to kill their enemies but to capture their horses and demonstrate their bravery as a means of winning prestige. An adult was esteemed according to personal loyalty to the people, generosity with his or her goods, kindness to the children, and bravery before enemy warriors. If any activity was not of the spirit, the wise elders said, it was not Indian. Life was so good they did not even know what mental illness was!

When a congregation loses its people and the ability to attract others, according to the Principle of Appropriate Rewards, it is revealing an inability to meet human needs. As I have said before, the motivation of men and women within a parish is not some mysterious element that we cannot understand. Every person is born motivated, lives motivated, and probably dies motivated—to do those things that are important. It is *prima facie* evidence that the church is functioning poorly when it does not win and keep members.

One of the mistakes I find pastors making in dealing with their members is a failure to perceive the causes behind their attitudes and acts. Behavior is never its own cause in an interpersonal relationship. Men and women do not do things *because* men and women do things. People hold attitudes and carry out actions because of internal and external factors and forces in their lives. The minister who focuses only on his or her own life and is unaware of the parishioners' motivations may not see the forces at work or may not understand their importance even if they are seen. But that does not make them any less real.

Babies do not cry in worship services without a reason. Neither do they cry because they are evil and trying to disrupt a sermon. Children do not usually run off with their friends rather than raking the leaves because they hate their parents. And few of your adversaries in the congregation are satanic or motivated by a desire to see your career fail.

The baby cries because it is hungry, bored, wet, or uncomfortable and seeks relief or satisfaction. Children neglect their chores because the interpersonal reward of playing with friends is temporarily more important than pleasing a parent. Some people in the parish oppose a minister because they have perceptions and goals that differ from those of their parish leader.

All attitudes and acts, including those that seem illogical and irrational to you, have an underlying cause. Even a mentally ill man in a hospital who walks over to another patient and hits her on the head with a chair is motivated by something that makes sense to him. What would *you* do if the radio receiver that the CIA implanted in your head told you that the woman was a dangerous enemy agent who was going to cut your throat as soon as you fell asleep? From his perspective, the most bizarre behavior is logical to him, if not to anyone else.

We seldom have such extreme people as that in our churches, but we do have disagreements and conflicts aplenty. Therefore, you must discover the attitudes, expectations, and mind-sets that perpetuate seemingly inappropriate views and actions. You must set the stage for positive attitudes, spiritual values, high expectations, and mature beliefs to be translated into responsible choices. In a sense this entire book is about that idea, but there is a principle you can follow to create a series of one-to-one rewards that powerfully influence people to do as you want them to. Of course, if you see yourself as a facilitator rather than as a parish leader, you may visualize your role as waiting until the congregation decides what must be done and then helping it reach its goals. I see that as an abdication of what you should be doing, for I believe leadership to be a dynamic, ongoing activity.

Modifying Behavior Through Rewards

To use rewards from the physical, psychological, and philosophical aspects of life, understand the following concepts:

The reward must be given as soon as possible after the appropriate behavior is produced.

The more the recipient values a reward, the more it will influence his or her behavior.

Rewards must be given only when the desired behavior is offered and withheld at all other times.

Some years ago, when Jonathan, my youngest son, was in high school, we started having difficulty getting him to worship services on Sunday mornings. Church attendance had become a tribulation to him for a number of reasons. In the first place, we had bought a home in another community, which separated him from the boys he had known in Sunday school. He also had a learning disorder that caused a reversal of some letters in his perceptions. This made it difficult for him to read aloud. Yet his teacher continued to nag at him to read aloud from the Scriptures every Sunday, despite our instructions to the contrary. In other words, my son was following the premise with which I started this chapter. Not only do people tend to continue those things that reward them, they also discontinue those things that displease them. There is always a cause behind every attitude and act, and it makes sense to the person involved.

I went to the religious-education director of the church and quietly had Jon transferred to another class with a more cooperative teacher. I also placed him in a simple behavioral-modification program that I designed. It started like this:

give the reward as soon as possible.

Our congregation holds two services, with the church-school program concurrent with the first service. Then we have a fellowship time between the church school/first service and the second service. That gave me the time needed to connect my son's reward closely to the action I wanted. During that interval, I took him to a deserted industrial park and let him learn how to drive.

That takes us to the second step in the process:

offer deeply desired rewards to people.

There was probably nothing I could give a teenage boy that pleased him more than driving lessons following the church-school program. For all year before his sixteenth birthday, I drove a short distance from the church building to an unused, off-the-road location where I let him get behind the wheel and practice his driving skills for half an hour before returning to the second worship service.

Although I will work harder for a thousand dollars than I will for a hundred, there are limits to offering money as a reward to me. No amount of money could draw me into selling narcotics or alcohol to others. I have become what I am, and—as Frank Herbert wrote in his *Dune* series—a man will die before he will become the opposite of what he sees as central to self. The rewards used to shape the attitudes and actions of people must be compatible with their image of self-hood, but they must be desired as well. For example, I do a great deal of speaking to community groups that pay me nothing in money but reward me greatly by allowing me to share my concepts about leadership, motivation, and performance improvement. Each of those groups gives me a token of appreciation such as a paperweight, a ruler, or a tote bag with the group's name on it. I always accept the memento and thank the person giving it, but they are not why I go to speak. Neither is the free lunch.

I go because it is important to me to have people hear my

message. So it was with my son and is with most men and women in each parish. With a strong-enough reward at the appropriate level of motivation, virtually any person's attitude or behavior can be shaped. You can see this in the enthusiasm and creativity with which contestants approach television game shows. The money is important, but the contestants are also striving for status and self-esteem. The home viewers play for such nontangible rewards, for they win no money at all and are the audience that keeps the shows on the air.

Finally:

grant the rewards only when the appropriate behavior is offered and withhold them at other times.

My son soon came to understand the *quid pro quo* of this approach. Being considerably brighter than Pavlov's dogs or Skinner's rats and pigeons, he discovered its validity the first time he skipped church school and bicycled over for his driving lesson. I quoted him a variation of "good things happen to people who *cooperate.*" He didn't get his driving lesson that day!

I am not sure how much lasting effect the lessons in the church school had on his moral and spiritual development, although my son is a fine young man some ten years later. My behavior-modification plan did have a lasting effect on his driving skills, however. He has not had a moving violation in ten years. That's better than *my* record, so Jonathan evidently learned something from the experience.

Activating the Reward Process

There are three steps to the process of selectively applying rewards:

1. **Articulate**—Tell people what you want them to do. Explain what the rewards are and how they may gain them.
2. **Consequate**—Connect the rewards to the attitudes or the acts by granting them according to the principles discussed above.

3. **Evaluate**—Take time to figure out what has taken
   place and explain it to the people involved. Tell them
   how they can do better.

Articulate. Harold Fassbinder was the senior pastor of a
large congregation in San Francisco. He was a few years from
retirement, and the three associate ministers were competing
for his job. It seemed to Hal that the younger pastors were overly
concerned with competition, rather than cooperating as he
wanted. He kept no records, but in his view the competition was
more frequent than the cooperation. Hal called a meeting, artic-
ulated his concerns, relating them to the overall well-being of
the church, and bided his time.

Consequate. After one confrontation, Hal called in the associate that had been the most cooperative and said: "John, I liked
the way you refused to be baited by Harry and Janet today. That
showed me real maturity on your part, so keep up the good
work." After that, John was less argumentative than before and
even somewhat smug about it. Because so much of our behavior
and our attitudes revolve around the concept of reciprocity, the
second or third time Harry and Janet launched an attack that
John ignored, they were forced to examine their relationships
with John. That pause in the competition gave Hal time to tell
both of them the same thing he had previously told John. Sepa-
rately, he said to each, "You're handling yourself better with the
others now. There's less time wasted in our meetings and less
duplication of effort. It shows a growing maturity, so keep up the
good work." Hal had reduced the conflict without crippling the
ambition that made all three good workers in the parish. He had
rewarded his associates for improvement and once again related
their performance to the mutual gains yet to be fulfilled.

Evaluate. Within two weeks, he later told me, the conflicts
had fallen to zero, for the associates had learned the limits the
senior pastor would accept. If his survey of results had revealed
that the conflicts were continuing, he would have needed to
increase the rewards in some way. In most such settings, however, the boss's approval is enough to win the desired behavior—
especially if he or she uses the Basic Principle of Interpersonal
Relationships and the concept of reciprocity to demonstrate desired behavior, rather than implying, "Do as I say rather than as
I do."

14

The Principle of
Conflict Management

As I reported from my research with a score or more pastors, the parish ministry is a battlefield in microcosm. You will have to deal with anger, confusion, misunderstanding, and conflicts of various kinds. I would like to state right up front in my consideration of conflict that not all disagreements are wrong and counterproductive. There come times when the church must take a stand against sin and evil, when men and women must struggle against individuals and organizations that are doing damage to society.

This is why so many in the church have spoken out against abortion-on-demand and why others, equally sincere, have opposed the reliance on nuclear weapons in an era when their use would destroy civilization as we know it. Just two years ago, the United Methodist Bishop of Minnesota, Emerson Colaw, came out in opposition to the building of a large horse-racing complex near the Twin Cities. I doubt that the bishop has anything against horses, but he did not want to see the introduction of pari-mutuel gambling, with all the accompanying evils that might follow—and that *have* now followed in its wake. Even the apostle Paul was willing to criticize and try to correct another's course of action when he felt it to be wrong and harmful to the church:

But when Peter came to Antioch, I opposed him in public. . . . he

drew back and would not eat with the Gentiles, because he was
afraid of those who were in favor of circumcising them.

Galatians 2:11–12

It is possible to avoid conflict at virtually any time and under
all conditions. All one need do to avoid disagreements is surrender to the demands made by others, never have any lasting
convictions, and obey as instructed. As a pastor, you would
thereby not have many conflicts, but you certainly would not
win any respect or exercise any lasting influence on the congregation either! The key to conflict management is to avoid and
control the *unnecessary* conflicts of parish life. These are the
little foxes that spoil the vines, according to Jesus, the petty
attitudes and choices that alienate others for no good purpose
save for one's own ego.

Many if not most unnecessary conflicts can be avoided by
using the Principle of Psychological Reciprocity that I discussed
in chapter ten. For the others that develop despite your treating
people as they should be treated, and for intervening in interpersonal conflicts that are not of your making, a good conflict-
avoidance process will prove valuable. The one I suggest here
will allow both parties to come away with half an emotional loaf,
since they will remain pretty much in their comfort zones.

This process will not solve everything, especially if the chairman of the official board is after your scalp or when someone is
threatening the well-being of your family, congregation, or community. You will then have to fight for what is right, rather than
obligingly surrender. The technique is very useful, however, for
those times when no great theological or philosophical issues
are at stake. It is based on the assumption that all emotions are
legitimate and necessary for survival and success.

Most deep-seated emotions are normal, although it is not
always appropriate to express them. It is appropriate to feel fear
at being nearly run over on the freeway or when being told that
your job is being phased out. Sexual desire is normal, since it not
only produces children for the benefit of the human race but
binds men and women together in a long-term relationship that
brings those children to a healthy adulthood of their own. Anger
toward people who are assaulting you physically or psychologically is also normal, for it has a survival quotient.

Because the vast majority of men and women know what I have just stated to be true, they will allow you the right to have your emotions—providing you do not use them to harm others. Because most people do this, you can use the three-stage process that Roberta and I developed in our book *Lovers for Life*. For one young minister and his wife, it worked like this.

Lois Benton, an oft-smiling supporter, had gone to considerable trouble to arrange a special Friday-evening meal for her pastor husband, Roger, in celebration of their three months of marriage. She had prepared gourmet food, and her anticipation of his pleasure grew as she imagined the meal together and the lovemaking that would follow later in the evening. Because she intended the meal as a surprise for her husband, however, she did not tell him about it in advance. And he, in all innocence and for the first time in their short marriage, failed to come home when she expected him. He stopped by the hospital for a last call of the afternoon, met another pastor, and got caught up in a conversation that made him lose track of time. He failed to call Lois, and no one knew where to find him when she checked with the church secretary.

As time passed and the dinner burned, Lois's anticipation turned to frustration and then to anger. By the time Roger finally wandered in, she was deeply distressed. When she complained, Roger the Controller failed to respond with any expression of regret and quite logically (to him if not to Lois) pointed out that he had known nothing about her plans. She, he continued, should have told him about the special dinner if she wanted him home on time. She replied that telling him would have ruined the surprise. He countered that it may have ruined the surprise but at least have saved the dinner.

He was greatly disturbed when his Supporter wife—who had long since slipped from her comfort zone and become tense—reached a high level of stress and attacked him ferociously. She lashed out at his attitudes, his values, and even his masculinity. She pointed out that her father, by whom she unconsciously measured all men, never did such a thing to her mother. Of course he had not; her parents had worked out such things long before she was old enough to understand what was going on!

Roger was deeply hurt by her attack, for even the most unresponsive Controller has the same emotions any other person does—Controllers just hide them better. He saw that attack as irrational and felt she had no right to berate him so. First he became autocratic, as Controllers tend to do when tense, and then he sullenly avoided her when his tension changed to stress. Some of their emotional intimacy was lost in the process, and it took several counseling sessions to learn how to use the three-stage conflict-avoidance process outlined below.

Levels of Communication in Conflict Avoidance

Stage One. Without resorting to personal attacks, calmly and openly reveal your feelings about what the other person has done to upset you. Use both words and nonverbal cues to authenticate your emotions to the other party. Avoid calling up past injuries—real or imagined—that may be completely irrelevant.

Lois, for example, has learned to say something like this when pressed from her comfort zone by something Roger has done, "When I work hard to do something nice and I don't know you'll be late, I feel that I'm not being treated fairly."

If Roger has listened carefully—as most people will do in any worthwhile relationship when not pressured by personal attacks or comparisons with others—he will remain in his own comfort zone. He will then tend to be openly communicative in return and make an honest attempt to change the behavior lapse that has upset his wife. Such a response will usually not only correct the specific conflict situation but improve the climate of the marriage itself.

Stage Two. On the other hand, the person responsible for causing the injured feelings may reject the complaint by ignoring it, by responding in a defensive and highly emotional manner, and/or by making no attempt to correct the original behavior. In the case of Roger and Lois, she would then be justified in increasing the intensity of stating her case. After all, she might reason, she had not attacked him personally nor assigned ulterior motives to him. She had merely exercised her right to reveal her feelings about the specific incident. Lois might then move on to a stronger, more explanatory approach:

> When you don't call, I become very upset about wasting my time and our money on something I have planned for our mutual pleas-

ure. I feel that I am not getting the cooperation I need to help keep my feelings for you strong and loving. That disturbs me very much, for I love you and want our life together to be all it can become.

With this approach, Roger would have to be a chowderhead to overlook her now-more-general message, but some people do just that for a variety of reasons. They may have selfish motives of their own or a psychological block that prevents them from listening to and understanding how others feel. Nevertheless, Lois has been emotionally honest in this stage, too. She has not made unfair comparisons, attacked his personal integrity, or questioned his motivation.

In many conflict situations, this second stage will bring about the desired results and strengthen the relationship through better understanding on both sides.

Stage Three: Here the ante is upped still further in intensity, and some sort of ultimatum is stated or implied. If, for example, Lois has still not seen any improved response to what she perceives as a valid complaint, she might now have to challenge the very nature of the relationship—especially if Roger persists in his superior attitude that *he* is okay and she is not. Lois might say:

When my feelings are not important enough to be considered, I become very angry with you. It upsets me so much that I feel like never preparing another meal for you, never making love to you again, not even living with you. In fact, the next time this happens—or anything like it—I'm going to leave this house as it is and go downtown to a show or something. That's how furious I become at being devalued like this!

Once again, Lois has avoided a personal attack on Roger and kept the focus on her own legitimate feelings. She is using the idea of reciprocity in a positive manner. Lois must be aware, however, that if Roger still refuses to cooperate, she will have to do one of two things. She must either accept and adapt to his ways without further complaint—or she must evaluate the marriage from this new perspective. Lois has issued a "threat," and implied in that ultimatum is asking herself whether the re-

wards of the marriage are enough from her point of view to
tolerate her husband's consistent devaluation of her feelings.

Although the third stage often brings results not obtained
through the other two, there are extreme cases where the
injured party may decide to end the relationship out of sheer
frustration, however devastating that may be in business,
church-related, or one-on-one situations.

You can teach your congregational members to use this three-
stage process in their dealings with each other, and it is powerful
indeed! It must be used *before* people are pressed too far from
their comfort zones, for once the behavioral shifts start to occur
according to personality patterns, full-blown conflict is much
more difficult to avoid.

Techniques of Conflict Control

Of course, there will be times when destructive conflicts grow
in intensity, regardless of how well you use the above process. In
that case, you will need some conflict-control techniques. The
best I have ever found are in the ASRAC process that you read
about in chapters seven and eight on member coaching and
counseling. After a conflict has started and someone attacks
you, your program, or another person in the parish, refuse to be
hooked into reacting as the attacker has. Tell yourself that someone must remain in a comfort zone to keep chaos at bay, that
someone has to remain the adult in the situation. And it might
as well be *you,* the one who has the knowledge that conflicts need
not run their course. Adapt the ASRAC process as follows:

ACCEPT the angry person's personality pattern with an open-
minded psychological attitude. Let him or her speak freely, without rebuttal, interruption, or criticism. Give the speaker verbal
and nonverbal permission to say what he or she feels with emotional honesty. Listen, listen, listen!

SHARE your understanding of how the speaker feels by demon-
strating your empathy and concern. Agree with the speaker in
those elements of the situation where it is possible to do so authentically: "Wow! If someone contradicted me without facts in
that situation, I would have felt angry also."

REFLECT your grasp of the situation by showing the speaker

what he or she is saying. Paraphrase angry words and put the speaker's unspoken emotions into words. You will have to interpret his or her nonverbal communication to do this. Say something like "Let me see if I understand you correctly. Feel free to correct me if I get it wrong." Paraphrase the previous statements to show how well you understand the situation and his feelings.

You should *pause* at this point, for you have been dealing with the angry person's emotions. (It makes no difference if the anger is directed at you or at some other person in the congregation.) By coming to grips with the emotions first, you will have a much better chance of getting the conflict under control. This break in the process allows time for the intensity of feelings to subside. Then go on to deal with facts:

ADD information, even if it was previously known to the angry one. This gives the person a *logical*, face-saving way to change his or her position. Since no one wants to appear manipulable or unreliable, additional facts permit a graceful shift in viewpoint. Always add new facts as a means of getting people to cooperate and change.

CONFIRM the results. This final step is to get the person, who has now experienced emotional catharsis, to come to realize that you do really understand. You have given him or her sound reasons to change and now ask for an agreement to let the matter be ended. Summarize the agreement and ask for confirmation in simple, supportive terms.

Conflict management is not easy, but it can be very effective when you use the three stages of conflict avoidance and the ASRAC conflict-control process shown above. You may find it valuable to return to chapters seven and eight and reread the section on the ASRAC procedure. Learn its principles thoroughly. Always deal with emotions first, even if you are a factual Comprehender, for you want to avoid placing people in such an emotional bind that they cannot cope with the facts of the situation.

When the great issues of life occur, as they did when Peter yielded to pressure and refused to eat with the Gentile Christians, you will have to go into combat with all your battle flags flying, as did Paul. But those occasions are few and far between.

Most conflicts arise from such less-noble issues as personal prestige and pride—power conflicts over who will be the choir director, sing the special songs in worship services, or the like. There
are so many messy human emotions that keep getting mixed up
in the eternal work of God's church! The better you learn to deal
with them effectively, the more successful you will be as a pastor.

15

The Principle of
Change Management

For roughly five thousand years of recorded history, we humans worshiped, worked, loved, and played in a relatively simple, static world that seemed virtually changeless. Every boy grew up knowing that he would be a hunter, herdsman, farmer or craftsman, as his ancestors had been and as his descendants would be. While they lived the kind of life recorded in the Old Testament, most people naively assumed that so would things remain until the end of time.

Each girl learned that she was going to spend her life gathering food, preparing and cooking it, making clothes, and having children to rear as her clan had always done. Life seemed changeless to our ancestors, and a shifting, restless society like ours would have been unfathomable to our not-too-distant forebears. People were surrounded by brothers, sisters, cousins, parents, and grandparents who lived in the same style, working from dawn to dusk simply to survive. Both sexes had their roles, and the purpose of much within religion was to keep people from dangerous experimentation.

> Do not conform yourselves to the standards of this world, but let God transform you inwardly by a complete change of your mind.
> Romans 12:2

How mistaken is our assumption that modern-day people

welcome change! Actually, most human beings resist it. One of
the most firmly entrenched traits of people everywhere is to
keep things as they were when they first learned them. We hate
change unless it is to our obvious and immediate advantage. We
see this tendency in our businesses, our schools, and in our
churches—and it can cripple us.

A growing number of social scientists now report that the
greatest danger to humankind is not the possibility of nuclear
war or the shortage of fossil fuels to run our civilization. It is,
they say, our resistance to change *when it is necessary*. For example, we of the industrialized countries have done pretty well
for ourselves in conquering disease, starvation, and poverty. Yet
our political leaders in Washington, London, Bonn, and Tokyo
profess not to understand why young men from desperately hungry nations become terrorists who attack us.

Our ancestors won their bread by the sweat of their brows
when life was indeed nasty, brutish, and short. Our laws, traditions, and economic system developed around the concept of
scarcity—we must fight to keep the have-nots from stealing
from the haves. In a time when we could perhaps feed the world
several times over, we fortunate ones can never again hope to
persuade the poverty-stricken nations from rebelling against
the status quo. They want "in." They want to access the world's
economic system *now*. If held out, the next generation of terrorists, or "freedom fighters," will be exploding nuclear weapons
rather than car bombs in the streets of industrialized cities.

Changes in the Church

As socioeconomic change floods in on us, we in the church
have trouble adapting. A few years ago, in the book *Lovers for
Life,* Roberta and I reported about a large, prominent congregation in a Minneapolis suburb that discovered nearly one-
third of its membership to be unmarried women. Some were
young and not yet married, some were divorced, some widowed,
but a significant percentage of this strong congregation was not
living the way that women have traditionally lived. We observed
that the church leadership had done little to meet the special
needs of nearly a third of its members. When I spoke to the
present pastor, I was unhappy to discover that little had changed

in the interim. A young woman minister had been added to the staff for a few years but is gone now, and the congregation has reverted to an all-male pastoral staff.

Churches that have experienced a stable emotional climate for decades recognize few reasons to change anything significant in their theology, worship, or outreach. Clergy and members alike see themselves as God's spokespersons to the world, and the temptation is great to rest on past laurels, to assume that life and Christianity will always go on in the special pattern we have inherited. In earlier days, except for far-flung missionary efforts, there was no need or way for congregations to reach out across the miles to deal with people *en masse* or individually. Congregations were made up of people who lived close to one hub of operations. Today, religious operations such as those led by Pat Robertson, Oral Roberts and Robert Schuller have ridden the crest of the electronic age and brought exciting changes to the church. Reaching out through the airwaves, they have kept the best of the personified relational Christian message and extended it exponentially by using the technology of our era. Obviously they are meeting the needs of many men and women, or they would not be so successful as they are. As a minister, you would be wise to examine today's resources and peer into the future to see what your congregation could be doing to become more effective under your leadership.

Facilitating Organizational Changes

There is a process for guiding change in an organization that goes back to the work of Kurt Lewin in the early nineteen forties. There are three stages involved:

Destabilize the status quo.

Create reasons for change to occur.

Restabilize at a new level of effectiveness.

As a preacher-pastor, you have a better opportunity to destabilize a group's comfort in a status quo than a business manager or a political leader. You have the bulk of the congregation in the pews every week to listen to your sermons. If you work

FIGURE 40 **Guiding Change in an Organization, Step 1**

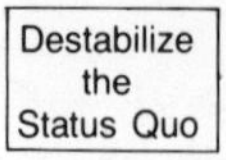

Destabilize the Status Quo

wisely and well, you can shift group opinion slowly but surely, until a demand wells up for which you just happen to have a solution.

Never make the mistake of being too subtle when rocking the boat. I did this in my first pastorate as a young minister. I used psychological techniques and a low-key approach for months as I tried to create a tidal wave of enthusiasm for a new church-school unit. This method produced not a ripple. Nothing happened! When my successor arrived, he began beating on doors, actively raising money while preaching the need, and soon had everyone anxious to move ahead on the project.

If you need to, reread the section on motivation in chapter three. Remember, I said that men and women do the things that are important to themselves—and little else. People work together to *have* desirable things, to *do* interesting activities, and to *become* participating citizens of the group. You must fit your preaching, your writing of parish newsletter articles, and your personal conversations with congregational leaders into that pyramid of *physical, psychological,* and *philosophical* motivation if you want to destabilize the status quo. This takes time and effort in virtually every situation, save for the roof blowing off, as I discussed earlier. You simply cannot go to the group and its leaders and say, "Change now because *I* feel it is better for the church." You may occasionally pull off something like that, but you are spending your leadership coin unwisely in doing so. Sooner or later people will revert to doing only what is important to them personally. When you influence the congregation to destabilize the status quo, the process begins to look like figure 40.

The reasons people perceive for change to occur will be embodied in your efforts to destabilize what it is you wish to change. One of the pastors I interviewed in my research took me to observe a lovely entryway of stone that had recently been constructed in his sanctuary. He told me how he had gone to the widow of a wealthy merchant who had worshiped in that church

Figure 41 **Guiding Change in an Organization, Step 2**

for years and suggested that she might like to use some of his estate as a lasting memorial in his name. He was giving her a reason to change something in her relationship with the congregation. She liked the idea and contributed many thousands of dollars to something very beautiful and conducive to worship in that sanctuary.

A couple I have known for years has gone to the Philippines to translate Scripture for the Wyclif organization. Donald and Jeanne DeLaCruz visited many congregations to raise support—financial, psychological, and spiritual—before they went overseas. They did an excellent job of offering the people of the different churches many grand reasons to make a change in not only their giving but also in their concern for other peoples and their own prayer lives. The Wyclif approach is much too sophisticated for my friends to have simply gone in to say, "Do things differently—to please *us*." They used films and literature and speakers that caught the interest and concern of the church members and drew them into something larger and possibly more important than themselves. Donald and Jeanne gave them a chance to *do* something important psychologically and to *become* people who care spiritually.

The process then looks like figure 41.

Finally, you must fix the changes at a new level of effectiveness and efficiency for the congregation. You want to internalize the new concept of calling, giving, praying, or whatever, establishing it firmly in the life of the church. Once again you have an advantage over a business or industrial manager, who is limited in the rewards that can be offered. You are working with the most important elements of life, so harness these motivations wisely. Confirm the worth of men and women who give of their time, talents, and money to accomplish purposeful and permanent activities. Teach them how to mature by growing from the simple *having* of things to the *doing* of important tasks for God and on to *becoming* what Christ would have them be. Offer people recognition and esteem as they grow in worth to the

FIGURE 42 **Guiding Change in an Organization, Step 3**

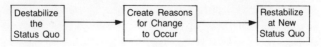

church and to God's world. Restabilize the congregation at a new
level of spirituality. Then your chart will look like figure 42.

The Pastor's Role in Change

I am convinced from my experience and research that very
little significant improvement will occur in a congregation without the wholehearted support of the pastor. Some changes may
occur as a result of laissez-faire neglect (including the name of
the pastor on the church stationery), but improvements seldom
will. In a larger parish, you may assign an assistant to carry out
the actual work—indeed you must, else you would be overwhelmed with administrivia and burned out fighting brush
fires. But even then you must be deeply committed to the work,
deeply involved in promoting it, and willing to give everyone
else credit for making things happen.

Lead and guide your associates and your people, but never
become manipulative. I knew a bank manager who wanted to
initiate a new balancing procedure despite the resistance of his
tellers. He pressured them and they refused, until in despera-
tion he began quietly dropping a few pennies or nickels in their
cash drawers from time to time. Of course, when they tried to
reconcile their funds, they could not do it. The figures were
always off, and the situation became so unstable that when the
manager suggested his plan again, the tellers jumped at the
idea. This approach worked, but it was manipulation. I shudder
to think what has happened to trust and mutual respect between the manager and his employees, especially if they discovered his Machiavellian approach to change.

If you would have people accept change willingly, you must
convince them that it is in their best interest to do so. Remember
the central fact of motivation: we humans do the things that are
personally important. Communicate to your associates and lay-
leaders the value of the change and then have a well-organized

and trained core group to follow up with the membership. Hold focus meetings to thrash out conflicts and confusion. Make the whole process a big affair that will benefit everyone in some way.

There is a psychological principle about human activities to be remembered at all times in managing change within your parish. When you set the stage for people to receive skimpy rewards from their fellowship, the church receives limited commitment. When average awards are received, average commitment is given. At this point, however, a new corollary takes over. When a congregation breaks free of the ordinary and the mediocre—and connects the rewards of membership to a deep Christian commitment—the church receives exceptional support in a wide assortment of ways.

Of course, Jesus taught this in the parable of the measure pressed down, heaped up, and running over, didn't he? I wonder why it has taken us so long to put his teachings into practice.

PART 4

Moving Toward
Church Growth

16

Local Evangelism

As I read and interpret the Scriptures, I discover that one great responsibility of committed Christians everywhere is to lead other men and women to a personal relationship with the Lord Jesus Christ. We are all called in the Great Commission to make the sharing of the faith a major part of our lives as Christians.

> Jesus drew near and said to them, "I have been given all authority in heaven and on earth. Go, then, to all peoples everywhere and make them my disciples: baptize them in the name of the Father, the Son, and the Holy Spirit, and teach them to obey everything I have commanded you. . . ."
>
> Matthew 28:18–20

When I was a young man preparing for the ministry after my return from military service following World War II, relational or evangelical Christianity seemed to have run its course. Not only had the concept of a personal encounter with God almost vanished from the world's churches, the future of Christianity itself was being called into question. Western civilization was badly crippled in the aftermath of two World Wars, the Holocaust, and the uneasy truce that followed. The church, which had been at the very heart of society for almost two thousand years, suffered along with other institutions of the civilized world.

A survey by one of my professors at Pasadena College led him to conclude that no more than two or three persons per hundred in Southern California were practicing Christians who had personally committed their lives to Christ. There was no doubt, even if his dismal figures were exaggerated, that the vitality that had long moved the church was largely lost. Certainly European Christianity—Protestant and Catholic—had so compromised with Fascist dictators that they lost a great deal of their influence. With the exception of a few like Martin Niemöller, that generation of church leaders failed miserably.

The Roman Catholic Church, for centuries a dominant force in the lives of most European citizens, reacted in an ineffectual manner to the political and social changes contributing to the events of World War II. Pope Pius XI, for example, in the interest of expediency, maintained a policy of neutrality toward the Fascist inroads of the Axis powers. With war imminent, his successor, Pius XII, likewise refused to confront the issue of totalitarianism and barely acknowledged the greatest evil of all time—the slaughter of millions in Hitler's "final solution," a horror that swept into oblivion Christians and non-Christians alike. Because of this hands-off policy, much of the church's financial assets and physical structures were preserved and pastors saved their skins, while others laid their lives on the line. Nevertheless, organized religion was burned in the trial by fire and emerged as a relatively inconsequential influence in postwar Europe. Even as rebuilding occurred, it was obvious that the church had lost its relevance. Only about one-half of one percent of European people attend regular services today.

Elsewhere the church has been more fortunate. Although buffeted by change and crippled by the existential frustration caused by a secular approach to life, New World Christianity has made a comeback. For the first time in four hundred years, the Latin American church has identified with the poor and needy rather than with the rich and powerful. The African church is exploding so that the geographical center of Christianity is expected to shift south of the equator by 2025. Overall, the church is probably in better shape than it has been since the great disillusionment caused by the 1914–1945 madness, which left its disfiguring mark on historical events ever since.

Some 35 to 40 percent of all United States citizens now testify that they have consciously come to Christ in a personal relationship. And why not? As Soren Kierkegaard wrote a century and a half ago at the beginning of the industrial revolution, it is only with a self-transcending faith in God that we can circumvent the pressures of our era. Of course, that still leaves from 60 to 65 percent of the people in most communities as candidates for local evangelism! Put your people to work in outreach, for we do indeed have a story to tell to the nations.

Enlisting Christian Responsibility

To build your church to a higher level of influence and attain all the good things that additional resources and relationships imply, convince your people that personal evangelism is both their right and responsibility. Demonstrate to them how they can succeed when they combine divine and human strength to tell the story of a redemptive lifestyle. Teach your men and women that they can take part in the great stirring now taking place within the church. Show them by your personal example that by sharing their faith with others, they will become more and more mature as Christians.

In setting up an evangelism program, you will have to use judgment, patience, and love. A few months ago I conducted a "Sharing the Faith" seminar, which comes from my book *The Psychology of Witnessing*. The program ran through several sessions at a fine church in Minneapolis. In the opening session, I asked for a show of hands by the people who found it difficult to testify to other men and women. After a count, I asked for those who found it easy to talk to others about religion to lift their hands. There was no contest. The people who found it difficult outnumbered the others by at least four to one. You will probably have to be at your most persuasive to recruit workers, but if you will read on in this chapter, you will find what is probably the best way to do visitation evangelism in your community.

Evangelism and the Three R's

I am convinced that most people who have had a spiritual restoration in Christ want to share their faith with others but, unfortunately, don't know how to go about it. Although, as a minister, you will not want to trade on their guilt to force them to do what they are not comfortable doing, the work must be done. Every Christian can witness, but while some are born anew as fishers of men, others must learn the skills needed. It is not enough to emulate the apocryphal barber who was converted on Sunday and could hardly wait for Monday morning to tell his story. He lathered his first customer for a shave, stropped his razor, and laid the cold steel against the man's throat. Eager to share his newfound faith, he paused and asked most sincerely, "Brother, are you ready to meet God?" According to the story, the customer was not! He bolted in panic. So do nonbelievers when Christians use more enthusiasm than skill in their personal evangelism!

The main reason many Christians dislike working as personal evangelists for the church is their fear of being hurt. Few of us want to be insulted, humiliated, or rejected, and we have learned that a great many men and women feel their religious beliefs are their own affair. They resent people they feel to be prying in something they consider just as personal as their sex life. I certainly do not recommend that you send out your evangelists to ask strangers, "Brother, are you ready to meet God?" or "Sister, are you saved?" I do suggest that you teach them how to use the Three-R process:

Relate warmly in love to develop friendship.

Recognize how people see their needs.

Recommend personalized solutions.

All people are ever hopeful that there is a more satisfying way of life open to them. Were this not so, the manipulative cults would not find such fertile ground for their distorted promises. Under his or her shell of cynicism, even the most skeptical person hopes that life can be better. We have only to develop a trust-filled relationship with others in order to have them listen to us and our message of Christ's redemptive power for their lives.

In *The Psychology of Witnessing,* I wrote that Christians should become outgoing spiritual counselors who work as personal problem solvers rather than salespeople who are peddling their own beliefs. The gospel is not a product to be sold but a relationship to be shared. There is first one's personal rela-

tionship with Christ and then new relationships in the congregation. Teach your people to use the Three R's as a means of
having others not only listen initially but want to hear more
about a better life.

Relate Warmly in Love to Develop Friendship. You want
to teach this first step of effective personal evangelism to your
people for two reasons. First, relating in love keeps one from
becoming manipulative and avoids confusing the ends with the
means. Second, by creating a friendly, trusting relationship
with another person, you pay your dues as a supportive comrade.
Friendship opens doors that nothing else can.

To illustrate, a few years ago I had to work with a man in
my parish whom I had found to be difficult. I knew that he is as
outspoken as I and that we have a personality clash and different philosophies of life. Because there was no way to get out of
working with Ralph Saunders, I made up my mind to use what I
know about relationships to defuse any conflict before it started.
I made a point of treating him fairly from the beginning. I asked
about his children and grandchildren and was courteous at all
times. When he fell ill, I sent cards and visited him in the hospital. I went out of my way to develop a strong interpersonal relationship. Sure enough, something changed in our interaction. I
found that Ralph was not an enemy but merely a strong man
who had his own convictions. We came to care about each other.

That happened because I paid my dues to him as a person
worthy of my esteem and trust. We still disagree on many
points, but when one speaks, the other listens. Ralph may not
yield, but we relate in friendship, and that gives me opportunities to persuade him that I would never have had otherwise.
Not long ago Ralph shook his head and quipped, "I must be
getting old. The things you say are beginning to make sense
some of the time!" Our friendship has made us both more aware
of the other's viewpoint.

Recognize How People See Their Needs. Teach your witnesses to get into their friends' personal frames of reference so
as to understand what is important to them. After all, each
person is unique in many ways. A canned, middle-of-the-road
approach is likely to be more often wrong than right. Simplistic
answers to generalized life problems will not mean much to

most people for one very real reason—no one will accept answers to questions he has not yet asked himself.

The best personal evangelist is a Christian who comes to recognize what is important to a friend and offers ways to meet his or her needs in Christ. The most effective way to learn what motivates other people is to ask questions about their lives and then listen to the answers given. If you ask indirect questions about spiritual needs and recognize the answers, a friend will reveal virtually everything you need to present the gospel in the best possible way. Until a witness has related warmly as a friend and then come to know what is important to the other, it is probably premature to say vaguely that Christ is the answer to life's problems. Moving ahead blindly is like shooting in the dark.

In a "Sharing the Faith" seminar recently conducted in a local church, I made the above point and a man argued with me. He said that all you had to do was to broadcast the gospel and let the Holy Spirit do the work. I had to disagree with him, for I have always shot many more bull's-eyes with a rifle than with a shotgun. I replied:

> Imagine that you are the president of a company that manufactures state-of-the art computers. Now imagine that you've been having a difficult time meeting the competition. Because of that, you decide to modernize to make better and less-expensive computers. I hear that you are buying all new manufacturing equipment, so I call on you and whip out my catalog and say, "I have just what you need to solve your problem. New anvils and hammers. If you buy thirty-five anvils and two hundred single-jackhammers from me, you will have the finest computer factory in the world. Let me sign you up right now, for that will solve your problems." What would you tell me?

The dissenter hesitated but finally admitted that my approach would make no sense to him in that case for one reason. *My* solution did not fit *his* problem.

This is precisely the case when counseling men and women to commit their lives to Christ. You must get deeply enough into their personal worlds to recognize what *they* need. Only when people start to question the wisdom of living as they have been, of going on without a personal relationship with God, will they start to listen to *your* answers to their questions about life.

Recommend Personalized Solutions. Teach your members how to recommend a personally meaningful aspect of Christianity to their friends, *after* they learn enough about their lives to make sense. For example, a Christian witness will seldom be effective by recommending Christ as a source of peace and tranquility to a youthful athlete striving for all-state honors. It is not what he or she needs. Neither would the witness be successful by offering Christ as a means of creativity and productivity to an elderly woman in a nursing home. Both individuals need a personal relationship with God through Christ, but each has interests that will have a specific effect on the things that would make the gospel meaningful and attractive.

Each witness must be honest and realistic when recommending personalized solutions to friends. By promising too much too quickly, the evangelist's efforts can lead to disappointment and frustration. After all, although most men and women are perceptive enough to realize that becoming a Christian will not resolve all of life's problems, some are not. Teach your people that the parish is a battleground in which men and women will be crippled or killed spiritually unless they are nurtured and made strong enough to resist attack. Commitment to Christ does not prevent business bankruptcies, keep people from losing their jobs to foreign competition, or eliminate the suffering in marital breakup. Some immature Christians may assume that they will be free from life's frustrations, but they simply have not been around long enough to know better.

Neither a physician nor a psychotherapist recommends a cure for a personal illness before diagnosing the problem. The same should be true with a spiritual problem solver. Human beings are too complex to be offered a simple canned approach to satisfaction in Christ. That would be like selling anvils to that computer manufacturer. He had no need for another person's made-to-preconceived-ideas solution. Be specific in order to improve the probabilities.

By *relating* in friendship, *recognizing* the needs as the friend sees them, and *recommending* a solution to specific problems, a witness to Christ's redemptive grace will be much more successful in leading others to Christ and to fellowship with a con-

gregation that is strong in the Lord and supportive of God's
work.

A Plan for Member Visitation

After your people learn how to use the Three R's of personalized witnessing about Christ, you must put them to work
using their knowledge. Develop a system that enables them to
bring people into the church, so that the gospel can be pro-
claimed and the benefits of congregational membership demonstrated. I will not try to crowd an entire book's content into one
section, when there are so many good books on church growth
available today. I will, however, describe one outreach program I
have used and taught because it is so effective as to seem mirac-
ulous. It involves four concepts: *Planning, Implementing, Rewarding,* and *Integrating.*

Your goal is to have a major impact on the community by
managing change successfully. Consider what I wrote about
people professing to like change when they seldom do. Also recall what I said about people being motivated to do the things
that are important to them, that reward them personally. Put it
to yourself: Are *you* willing to work the next thirty-seven holidays so *I* can have a new sailboat? I thought not! Nor am I
especially interested in giving up my free Saturdays so you can
have a thriving career. Of course, the way men and women feel
about themselves has a powerful influence on their emotions
and actions.

In World War II, four Navy chaplains aboard a sinking cruiser
gave their life-preservers to seamen scrambling up from the
engine room. All four drowned as a result, and it is this intangible motivation of true Christians that can be used to put men
and women to work as "car pastors" in a powerful calling program. To activate change, you want your callers to destabilize
the status quo for the families they call on, to give the people
reasons to change, and to restabilize them at a new level of
satisfaction. I wrote about this process in some detail in chapter
fifteen. Review it if necessary to better understand what I am
recommending here.

Planning. Begin your growth program by convincing your
people that it is important to reach out in the community for

Christ. Get your ducks lined up well in advance—at least six
months—so your commitment and concern can percolate
through the entire congregation and be multiplied many times
over. Become a leader of the parish rather than simply a facilitator who suggests that things might be better. Work through
the cloverleaf pattern shown in chapter one. Make full use of
your resources and your relationships.

Don't be so naive as to think that everyone in the congregation will share your desire to bring people to Christian
commitment and personal service. There will be some who are
lazy, others who are too fearful to venture out into the community with Christ's invitation to "bring the little children" to him.
After all, by making public our profession of grace, we increase
our visibility and become possible targets for critics. Worst of
all, there will be some people in the parish who want things just
as they are. They want to remain large frogs in a small puddle
and know very well that growth will surely upset the status quo.
Regardless of who we are, each of us can find logical-sounding
reasons and scriptural passages to justify what we want from
life and our relationships.

I have heard arguments that an evangelism/visitation program would make the church look ambitious in the community,
would not be cost effective in accounting terms, and would attract the wrong kind of people. You must work around such
excuses, ignore them, or steamroller them if necessary. Refuse
to be stopped by the nay-sayers who will certainly be with you
all through your ministry. Preach from the Scriptures and from
church history about the happy rewards of strong congregations.
Teach that Christians do not find spiritual satisfaction by *seeking* spiritual satisfaction. Fulfillment in Christ always comes as
a by-product. Individuals are happy in Christ only when they
have legitimate cause to be satisfied. A congregation, too, must
have its reasons to be satisfied, and winning others to Christ and
the church is the best single way I know.

Raise parish expectations from the pulpit. Write pieces for the
midweek mailer or Sunday bulletin. Tell about other churches
that have become great in their outreach. Lead programs that
demonstrate what can be accomplished through faith and
works. Set high goals that build on positive expectations and
strong spiritual values. Teach the members to express powerful

affirmations of what they will do cooperatively to obey the Great Commission of Christ.

Implementing. Prepare your people to expect great things as you recruit a group of them to share your vision. These will be your "car pastors." Each will first pledge to give the church a half-day in which to learn and a half-day for a trial run. Anyone who can drive a car safely, talk to children comfortably, and speak to parents for a few minutes is able to work this program successfully. They will also have to commit an average of one hour per week after training to keep the program going. Put some of your best people on this, for you want the prestige to be high. Make your itinerant pastors the most important members of your congregation.

Prepare for the trial visitation well in advance. The preparation must include the following:

1 *Print enough instruction sheets for each car pastor.*
2 *Collect an assortment of balsa gliders, paper-doll books, balls, and other inexpensive attention grabbers such as church-school comics and story sheets.*
3 *Divide the community into convenient squares and mark them on a large-scale city map.*
4 *Issue church calling cards in sufficient numbers.*
5 *Print enough badges and official authorization sheets for the car pastors.*
6 *Pair the car pastors two to an automobile, with one person being the primary witness and the other the back-up.*

Conduct the training seminar from 9 A.M. to noon, have lunch together, and then go out to implement the calling program around 1 P.M. Start the seminar portion promptly and lead it personally to demonstrate its importance to the congregation.

Begin by teaching them in a simplified form the Three R's of good witnessing previously outlined. Pair the participants as they will be going out and let them practice some scenarios using the Three R's. Teach them how to *relate* in friendship and give them some examples to follow in their role playing. Do the same with *recognizing* and with *recommending* solutions. Talk about the Three R's and then answer questions. If you need it, get a copy of my book *The Psychology of Witnessing,* which is still in print as this book is being written. After a short break, say at 10:30, introduce the participants to the actual calling portion of the program.

Start by handing out instruction sheets upon which the following is written:

> Drive down the street in your assigned sector of the community and look for signs of children at each home—bicycles and trikes on the sidewalk, basketball hoops over the garage doors, swings in the back yard—whatever tells you that children live in that house.
>
> If you see children out and about, ask them to take you to their front door to meet their parents. Ring the bell or knock, (even if the child invites you in) and await the parent on the outside. If there is no child around, ring the bell and speak to the parent who answers.
>
> Identify yourself as a visitation worker from your church. Display your badge and hand the parent your identification card or form. Explain that the church is starting a bus route for church-school-age kids and that you would like permission to pick up their kids the following morning (or whenever the next session is). Describe the kind of program to be offered, give parents some of the sample materials, and be friendly enough to establish a good rapport. Tell who the pastor is and who the church-school workers are. Invite questions from the parents.
>
> With the parent's permission, if the children are present, give them a balsa glider or a paper-doll book and a sheet of the school's comics or whatever you have in your bag that is appropriate. Ask if they would like to attend the program with other kids from the neighborhood. Stress the fact that this is a neighborhood program for local children.
>
> Ask the parent for permission to pick up the children at the appropriate time and return them home at a prearranged hour. Stress the fact that you as the church visitation worker will be present from door to door.

Explain to your volunteers that more parents than they would believe possible will simply give them permission on the spot, although some will call the church office to verify credentials. This is why each car pastor should carry a supply of church

cards. Other parents will say that they belong to other churches
and that their children are already active in church schools.
Great! The visitor should thank them and go to the next house
that reveals signs of children. If parents just say that they are
adult members somewhere else, the volunteer might ask
whether the children attend each Sunday. If they hesitate or
admit that the children do not attend regularly, here is where
the car pastor should take the advantage for Christ!

The immediate goal is to persuade the parents, in the best
manner, that the church bus provides a convenient way for them
to see to the children's spiritual training. This will give them an
extra two hours to relax or read the paper or whatever. Remind
the visitors to relate to the parents and recognize what might
motivate them to give permission to have their children taken to
church school.

When you recognize people from your own congregation, tell
them what you're doing and ask the children if they have neighbors with whom they would like to be seated.

In either case, with permission or without, the visitation people must keep records about the call on 3×5 cards that are
filled out when returning to the car. The volunteer should list
the street address, try to record the family name, the names of
the kids, and the results of the visit. One refusal should not be
the end of it, for the church will be able to get enough youngsters
to start a route, and in time the family can be approached
again—often with more success once a visitor has become a
neighborhood phenomenon! I have seen many kids waving goodbye to a car pastor and running home to persuade their parents
to let them go the following Sunday.

You might also distribute to the volunteers another set of
rules for pickup and return:

> Buy a pair of magnetic plastic signs that attach to the car doors
> when pressed there. Identify the car as the Berean-Baptist or the
> Longview-Lutheran Church School Bus.

> Arrive somewhat earlier than expected, for you are changing a
> long-established pattern and the kids might still be in bed. Give
> them time to get ready and tell the parents to forget breakfast
> because cookies and milk or juice will be available at the church.

Observe safety limits, but fill your car. I once had thirteen little kids in a Renault Dauphine, although I don't recommend it.

Give everyone a great time with trained teachers and exciting activities and get them home on schedule.

Deliver each child to his or her door and ask whether everyone had a good time. Tell the child you'll be back next Sunday morning. After a few Sundays, begin alternating with the back-up car pastor so you will not always be late for church services.

Work your route often enough to keep the car filled and get helpers to pick up the extra children you may recruit as time goes by

Check with your insurance company and make sure there is adequate liability coverage to protect yourself, the children you transport, and the church in case of accident. Better yet, have the activity covered by the church's liability policy.

This is a fantastic church-school growth program. I have seen churches that sent out fifty or sixty car pastors on a Saturday afternoon and recruited three or four hundred new prospects for the next day. One church in Oklahoma City used this program for three months and brought in thirteen hundred new families. Obviously the car pastors will have to return to the church after their initial calling session. Line up a crew ready to sort the cards and alert the teachers that a mob is coming. Have a serving team for juice and milk and cookies. Be sure there are enough teaching materials. It is the church's responsibility to have everything ready to justify such effort. In the debriefing session after the trial run, ask for shared suggestions from the car pastors and have them share war stories about suspicious parents, angry dogs, and successful relating used to bring about the parents' permission. Plan on meeting once a month until the program has been integrated into the congregation's activities. Appoint a prestigious church leader to oversee the car pastors and make it an honor to do the work.

Rewarding. There is a point to the effort, of course, and that is to win people to Christ and the church. Let me say this again, for although everyone knows it, all too few pastors practice it: *People are motivated to do only those things that are important to themselves.* Your goals can only be reached by giving more and more people legitimate reasons to commit their lives to Christ

and serve the church in fellowship with the rest of the congregation.

Reward the workers with prestige; give a dinner at which
they are the honored guests. Reward them physically with
scrolls and ribbons, reward them psychologically with recommendations and praise, and reward them spiritually with blessings from God's Word. Actually the three kinds of rewards—
physical, psychological, and spiritual (or philosophical)—are as
mixed in a person's perceptions as the ingredients of a cake after
it is baked. Touch on all three aspects to be sure each participant
receives recognition.

You and your staff—both professionals and lay-leaders—
should reward the children, too, with good teachers and programs that connect to the church year in many ways. Give them
nice things to talk about when they go home. Let them take part
in programs and plays. Have special visitors' and children's worship Sundays. Use your sanctified imagination and collective
talents to make it all worthwhile. Reward the parents of the new
children by showing them what their kids are doing in plays and
the programs. Involve the parents by asking them to make cos-
tumes, and insist that they come see their kids in operation.
Remember how successful Professor Harold Hill was in *The Music Man* with his Think Method? The parents were screaming in
pleasure at the end.

Integrating. I know of entire United Methodist Conferences
that have sharply turned around a long-term membership loss
by working through the church school to bring the parents into
fellowship with the congregation. That is not the end, however,
but just the beginning. The secret is to integrate the results of a
successful church-school growth with the long-term goals of the
congregation.

A minister and a congregation should work from a well-
balanced plan of operations for the long haul. It is most certainly
overall healthy growth that we of the church are interested in!
The long-range plan, however, should never be so rigid that it
forces people into predetermined tasks and roles. Men and
women are simply too complex to fit into my mold—or yours, for
that matter. That is where a multilayering approach is so valuable. Your car-pastor program, for example, must be ongoing yet

mesh smoothly with other outreach endeavors and subject to revision as changing circumstances require.

Flexibility in Outreach

Be your own best example of a flexible Christian leader who is able to adapt to the inevitable changes of our era without being unduly disturbed. After all, the church is to be an agent for change in society—leaven in the loaf of life, light in the darkness, and a city set on a hilltop to guide weary travelers. Jesus' analogies are still harmonious with life. In the car-pastor example, go out *before, with,* and *after* your visitants to keep your finger on the pulse of the entire community. Call on everyone you can, but be especially persuasive with successful middle managers, physicians, teachers, and the other professionals of a neighborhood. They are often the people who will do the best work for a church. Handpick the car pastors for those neighborhoods where the leading achievers of the community live, and persuade them to invest a portion of their lives in attaining goals that will never be lost. Demonstrate to such people that they can meet their needs in the congregation by doing what interests them and by bringing others to work with them.

Not long ago a pastor friend of mine brought in a young physician, his wife, and their two children through a community calling program. The young man served about five years and then took a sabbatical to donate six months of his time working through his denominational office in Kuala Lumpur, Malaysia.

Consider the following suggestions for broadening your church's outreach activities, but remember that there are virtually unlimited possibilities.

1 *Find someone who is a chess nut and have him or her form a chess league among the community's churches.*
2 *Persuade a group of people to run a hamburger and chili stand at the county or state fair.*
3 *Let an outdoors enthusiast start a church-based hiking or mountaineering club and recruit members for it.*

4 *Start a Bible class that compares two or three translations and thereby finds better ways to live.*

5 *Recruit men and women who are dedicated to scouting and have them start new programs for the boys and girls.*

6 *Enlist a building contractor to design and help build a church camp along a nearby river.*

7 *Find a local writer who will begin a literary group that reads books and meets once a month to discuss them.*

8 *Begin a self-help group for inner-city youngsters and finance a worker to help them make it through the difficult years.*

9 *Encourage a teacher to help your high-school students form a debating club so they can better deal with cult recruiters.*

10 *Persuade someone with the needed business or counseling skills to start a club of men and women who have lost their jobs and need support while starting over.*

11 *Organize a study group that uses The Psychology of Witnessing to help the church grow.*

There is no way to anticipate in advance the potential interests of a hundred or more men and women who come into the church with a fresh commitment to Christ. Because of this diversity, you must take them as they are, find ways to help them mature in the faith, and set them to work at things that interest them personally. Along the way, you can build a community of believers who will serve God and humankind better and better every day.

17

A Community for Spiritual Living

The apostle Paul never knew the kind or size of congregations that we have today, but the topics about which he wrote are timeless. Although the congregations to which he wrote letters were small, led by lay pastors, and met in private homes, the messages Paul sent remain valid for us today. He not only saw the church as it was but in light of what it could become for all time. His entire multi-faceted message to each congregation was for it to become part of a network of centers for spiritual living.

> Since you are God's dear children, you must try to be like him. Your life must be controlled by love, just as Christ loved us and gave his life for us as a sweet-smelling offering and sacrifice that pleases God.
>
> Ephesians 5:1–2

In his book *Pastoral-Care Counseling,* Howard Clinebell wrote that the purpose of the church is to improve the quality of life for the members. Rather than remaining self-centered, however, Clinebell takes a broader view of the good life than is normally considered. He writes the following about the work that a Christ-centered congregation should accomplish:

> The mission of the Church in the eighties and nineties is to be an *abundant life center,* a place for liberating, nurturing and empowering life in all of its fullness in individuals, in intimate relationships and in society and its institutions.

227

It should be obvious that this task requires more and more of the church as society becomes ever more complex.

When I was a boy, my parents took my sisters and myself to a little white frame meeting-house that was the spiritual home for no more than a hundred people. My mother and father seemed to be quite comfortable there as they taught classes and served in other ways. Unlike most of the farm and small-town families we knew, we traveled quite a bit. When we were away from home, often in large cities, we usually worshiped in large churches. My parents did not find this a satisfying experience, although my sisters and I loved it. I can now understand why they felt one way and we felt another.

My parents came from a community congregation in which everyone knew everyone else. They were accustomed to a small fellowship group for whom the morning worship service and the evening evangelistic sermon were virtually the only activities that occurred regularly. Once in a while we had a picnic or a revival meeting, but there was no singles' ministry, no Bible-study classes, and no charitable outreach into the community. To my parents and the other adults of the congregation, that was Christianity. They did not understand the concept of a large spiritual-life community in which public worship was only the tip of an iceberg of activities and relationships. They unconsciously expected to relate to people they met around the back of the sanctuary in the large churches as they did at home. When that did not happen, they complained that these churches were cold and formal. And my parents were among the most sophisticated and educated in the community!

We kids, however, loved the junior church services geared to our interest level, the well-trained and -equipped teachers, and the varied programs with a youth director or minister. It really spoiled us for the little church at home when we returned after a visit away. My parents simply never remained around the large city churches long enough to discover that a new world of complex activities and relationships would have been available for their spiritual growth.

Positive Reinforcement in the Church

I still hear people from small, often struggling, congregations saying virtually the same thing that my parents did half a century ago. They are accustomed to congregations that offer personal friendship and acceptance to those who already attend (providing they accept the local social customs), but they seldom reach out to anyone who is different from a rather narrow norm. Such churches do serve their members, of course, but they fail to realize that more complex congregations have a distinct advantage over them because of their multi-layered programs that meet many more different kinds of needs. Remember what I said about motivation—that people are moved to do the things that are personally important to them.

I am convinced that spiritual-life centers are precisely what the successful congregations I researched for this book have become. Without exception and in every case! They became strong enough to attract enough committed people to carry out their complex, growth-enhancing programs regardless of the denomination or theological bent. In fact, when I talked to the rank-and-file members, I soon discovered that they cared relatively little about the pastor's theology when he was proclaiming Christ as Redeemer and Sanctifier of the abundant life. Those congregations had found ways to make it worthwhile for people to come, to get to work, and to remain. Today's church has run headlong into a psychological principle called positive reinforcement by mental-health professionals of all persuasions.

The concept of reinforcement is simple. Normal people of all ages continue the activities and relationships that satisfy them and discontinue those that do not. When a congregation continues to grow, it is doing more things right than wrong for its community. When it continues to lose members, it is doing more things wrong than right. Everyone knows about reinforcement. My four-year-old granddaughter knows to crawl up on my lap to hug and kiss me after I give her a quarter. Even my dog comes around to lick my hand and wag his tail appreciatively after I feed him. I have never known a normal, healthy person who did not prefer a pat on the back to a kick in the seat of the pants.

The greatest mystery of my life as a leadership consultant is why so many managers, parents, teachers, and pastors ignore this simple fact of human motivation. We too often put people to work as though they were machines and then profess to be surprised when they malfunction from neglect. Although few admit it in government, business, or industry, this is one of the major

causes of the problems in which the United States currently
finds itself in regards to world trade and other areas of national
concern.

The concept of positive reinforcement must be a major factor
in your efforts to develop a community for spiritual living in
which people find consistent satisfaction. A pastor can use the
visitation concepts taught in the previous chapter or the more
deliberate methods taught by someone like Herb Miller in his
several books about church growth. They will all succeed when
the members are wisely led to do the work of reaching out in the
community. The world's oldest management cliché remains
valid today. The operative word is work! **Plan your work and
work your plan**.

To bring people in, you will have to reward them in some way.
To keep them you will have to be more sophisticated. The activities of the congregation must address the universal need of
men and women to *worship, work, love, play,* and *persevere*. In
the growth style of the fifties, a church could get away with
signing people up in their homes, proclaiming them Christians
and Methodists/Presbyterians/Episcopalians/Catholics/Baptist
or whatever. Parish leaders persuaded a great many families to
sign the order blank, but all too many of them failed to stop by
and pick up the product. We saw them only at Christmas and
Easter and for funerals and weddings. It is largely their children and grandchildren who have vanished from the rolls and
caused the slippage in membership among the main-line denominations today.

That kind of evangelism is all over now, for families ask,
"What's in it for us?" Unless people expect to receive satisfaction
from belonging, they just won't join. And if they do, they contribute little of value or they simply move on.

On the other hand, all people have the "spiritual unconscious" that Viktor Frankl discussed in his books. Humans have
cosmic needs that cannot be met through bigger and better
lawnmowers and speedboats on the lake. We need to feel at home
in a vast and uncaring universe. Better yet, we need to see that
the Creator is not cold and uncaring and that the universe is a
warm and accepting home for those who adapt their lives to the
Creator's principles of life.

A great deal of contemporary research shows that people are

deeply interested in religion and the church, that they will come
if invited and will join congregations that meet their needs.
Most men and women not currently members of a congregation,
however, are not bound by denominational traditions. Location,
kind of program, and congregational support are more important to them than theology or worship customs. These people
can be reached and they will join, but the programs must be
personalized for them. Because such people have discovered that
they cannot live well on bread alone, only a church that functions as a rewarding life-enhancing center will attract and keep
them.

Spiritually Balanced Congregations

The Christian life becomes truly meaningful to a person
when he or she makes a personal commitment to the Lord Jesus
Christ. I simply cannot see that anything less than a spiritual
restoration is sound theology or psychology. No athlete, artist,
manager, physician, teacher, or entrepreneur becomes the best
he or she can be without a personal commitment to excellence.
Likewise, congregations do not become world class by holding
ordinary values, attitudes, and expectations.

Convince your people that it is their duty as maturing Christians to share the faith with others. And when the newcomers
arrive, be sophisticated enough to offer programs that lead to
their spiritual growth. You certainly do not want to feed them
the same kind of pap about black people, Indians, unfortunate
welfare recipients, and our world competitors that they could
pick up in a blue-collar saloon! You will have to work at educat-
ing your people to help the newcomers. In fact, research reveals
that a call by a lay couple on visitors within two days after they
first attend the Sunday service is the best way to get them to
return. For every day after the initial two days, the percentage
of success drops dramatically. Strangely enough, a pastoral call
is not nearly as effective. It is as if the visitors feel the pastor is
paid to come and the lay callers are not. Apparently the lay call
is interpreted as an outreach from a congregation that really
cares. Teach your people this, and then set up a calling system
that reaches newcomers within two days—if you are really interested in numerical strength.

FIGURE 43 **Foundation Stones of Christianity**

In the companion work to this book, *The Emotionally Mature Christian,* I point out that the entry point to a spirit-filled life is a spiritual restoration that is variously called "being born again," "accepting Christ," or "making a commitment to Christ." In that book I try to spell out the differences between a spiritual awakening in Christ and the development of mature Christian discipleship. Such a distinction is important, for church programs and the commitment of always-limited resources will be different according to our goals. Birth is but the first step in maturing.

As a pastor, your responsibility in bringing men and women to sound discipleship must be focused through a balanced congregational ministry. The successful pastors I interviewed told me that they refused to let special-interest groups sidetrack them into a narrow vision of Christianity. I discovered that a balanced parish ministry rests on three major facets of Christianity. They are the foundation stones of Christian faith—SALVATION, SOCIAL ACTION, and SELF-HELP.

In a diagram they look like figure 43.

The *salvation* aspects of Christianity are the ones emphasized by Billy Graham in his public ministry. Here the focus is on making peace with God through an acceptance of the Lord Jesus Christ as personal Savior. This is the launch pad of all that follows, but it is not the only major thrust of a personalized spiritual approach to maturity. To focus too exclusively on this aspect of spirituality is to fail in the development of a well-rounded congregational mission as it is defined in Scripture and church tradition.

The second cornerstone of a maturing congregational mission is the *social action* aspect of the gospel. This is the part of the Christian message emphasized by Elton Trueblood in his books and by Jesse Jackson in his drive for voter registration, fair housing and job laws, and a great deal more help for blacks and other minorities. It is based on the scripturally confirmed belief that I am *indeed* my brother's keeper. It is reinforced by the fact that in the parable of the good Samaritan Jesus forever set the standard for our responsibility to our neighbors. Social action, although vastly unpopular in some branches of the church today, is as sound a ministry within the church as salvation.

The third aspect of a spiritually maturing approach to Christian fulfillment, as an individual or as an entire congregation, is the *self-help* approach. This is the major emphasis of Robert Schuller in his local and national ministry. It is as valid a Christian concept as salvation and social action, for all normal men and women are interested in becoming what they can be in the physical, psychological, and spiritual or philosophical aspects of life.

These three foundation stones deal with our relationships with *God,* with *others,* and finally with *ourselves.* Each is valid and each is growth-producing, although it is a mistake to get off the track and emphasize any one aspect at the expense of the other two. It is here that so many congregations get into trouble, unless the pastor is wise and strong enough to lead them well. A common mistake among the members of every religion is to assume that the culture in which they live and the religion through which they worship are the same.

There are hundreds of weekly radio programs proclaiming that Christianity *is* Americanism and vice versa. Some go so far as to teach that capitalism is Christian and that socialism is anti-spiritual. We always face the temptation to convince ourselves that what is best for ourselves is God's will for everyone else. Actually, the early disciples were quite collective in practice, and the church succeeded for centuries before capitalism was invented. There is no one approved Christian economic system given by God.

God's best work is always done by men and women in a balanced ministry. It is people, rather than procedures, that do the good work, although sound methods will help get the work done. Service to others—expressed through a salvation orientation, social action, and self-help—remains the only reliable method to reinforce the attendance of newcomers in a Christian church. Salvation is the entry, but a great many injustices remain to be cleared away, and we all need to improve ourselves in a variety of ways.

Building on Love and Acceptance

I am always surprised and a little shocked when I hear a minister confuse cultural mores and traditions with Christianity. This is a strange reaction on my part, for I know full well that a person's psychology influences his or her Christianity far more than religion influences the psychology. A person who lives with a negative mind-set sees everything in gloomy terms. Anyone who suffers from basic distrust and cynicism will fight to keep what little good is seen in life and freeze out all those other people who "cannot be trusted"—precisely as learned in childhood, when trying unsuccessfully to cope with too many pressures. As an adult, the person's theology and practical religion will reflect this negativism, even if he or she enters the ministry!

Several years ago, pollster George Gallup spoke about his personal commitment to Christ. As a devout Episcopal layman, he also said that if present trends continued, in twenty years or so there would be two kinds of churches in his denomination. There would be evangelical churches and dead churches. I suspect that his prediction was correct, although many of the changes he recommended are already taking place.

It is only as Christians become Christ-centered that we have any claim to spiritual legitimacy. It is in communion with Christ that we begin our growth toward maturity, continue it, and bring our lives to what they can become. This is true for individuals and for congregations. It is not especially easy to influence a group of diverse-minded men and women to work well together toward tangible and intangible goals that often contradict a variety of world views. But the basic theme of the gospel—the thread that can bind these variously motivated individuals into one unified fellowship—is the love and acceptance exemplified in Christ.

I find it necessary for a minister to use symbols as a means of sharing this vision and capturing member interest. There is nothing wrong with symbols and illustrations, of course. Jesus did his best teaching through parables, and Martin Luther said that one might as well try to scale walls without ladders as to reach heaven without illustrations. It is therefore essential for you to use the human need for symbolism to focus on new goals or the recasting of old goals in new ways. The rank-and-file members do need their ladders, and they will seldom reflect the same motives that move you. Some of the most successful media stars of the church have discovered this.

A number of radio and television religious stars picture themselves in a great American crusade to save the nation from Communists who are purportedly ready to invade San Francisco or El Paso if their ministries are not supported continually by a large number of people. A great many ministers have learned that, for men and women with a negative mind-set, fear sells better than hope. Fear, however, is the little death that destroys all that Christ tells us to become. The apostle John wrote most eloquently that love brought to fruition in Christ casts out fear and perfects our interpersonal relationships.

By contrast, Oral Roberts and Robert Schuller, in their equally visible ministries, have not chosen the easier, lower road for support by people caught up in the existential frustrations of our era. Nevertheless, they also use symbolism and easily understood concepts to gather a following within the electronic church. For example, Roberts's City of Hope campaign caught the imagination of literally millions of men and women because the vision of healing as a physical, psychological, and philosophical synthesis is understood and appreciated by people with a positive world-view.

You may be able to draw together a large number of people by appealing to their baser emotions, but their being assembled together will not make them a community of maturing Christians by any means. All it does is perpetuate the group's weaknesses by giving them an appearance of legitimacy. To succeed in all three aspects of a meaningful, maturing faith, you must take the initiative in the parish. You must share the long-term Christian principle that our loving God has called his people to leave childhood behind.

As my successful pastors told me in half a dozen different ways, get your theology straight that Christ is indeed Redeemer, Sanctifier, and Healer of the men and women who struggle for wholeness in this era of incessant change and confusion. God majors in changed lives, not in maintaining a cultural status quo that builds on fear, for it is fear alone that leads to racial, religious, and national prejudice. I know that it is easier to collect a crowd by running down the street in the dark shouting "Fire!" than to persuade them to donate their Saturdays toward building a playground for needy children. But any parish that drifts away from love for the members, an acceptance of other people, and a desire to have a positive influence on the world needs some stern Christ-centered leadership.

It is not enough to love only those who love us. Christ had a great deal to say about that in regard to the Pharisees. The ultimate test of discipleship comes when we are asked to love those who do not care about us. I fear that our congregations need a lot of gospel preaching and teaching in this aspect of following Christ.

Some of the biblical analogies compare people to sheep who have strayed and who need a shepherd. Others tell us that people are often like children. That is a good comparison, for we now know that we humans—indeed, all of creation—are some transitional aspect of stardust. "In the beginning"—there was hydrogen, and through God's marvelous alchemy the universe became the seed bed for life. (I cannot be so egotistic as to say that the cosmos became the seed bed for only humans.) We are the brawling, fearful, selfish children of the stars. We could have made the earth a paradise but instead have pressed it and our civilization to the brink of extinction because of our immaturity. Even yet, the outcome of man's world is in doubt.

In Christ, however, we are given the opportunity to leave the fears and hatreds of childhood behind. Through a spiritual restoration and with a maturing lifestyle, we can stop being childish in our values, attitudes, expectations, beliefs and choices. We can become God's *adults*! Paul tells us to do so in a hundred different ways. Teach that to your congregation. Find a myriad of ways to move them past the paranoia and fear that will surely cripple their growth, invade the church with a negative mindset, and limit your ministry. Perfect love—Christ-like love—casts out fear, and you must never stop preaching that.

Different pastors, like all normal humans, will automatically and unconsciously emphasize the aspects of the Christian life that best meet their personal needs. That's not good enough, for a strong leader is also a loving congregational servant. In my business consulting, I have found all-too-many companies in desperate straits because they persisted in making and selling buggy whips when their customers had sold all their horses! It is necessary, even as we have our own personal interests in the salvation, social action, and self-help aspects of Christianity, to focus consistently on the love and acceptance of people everywhere. Christianity at its best is never an insular experience but a reaching out from a life-enhancing center to do things for others.

I have felt this most strongly in vastly different places where my heart was stirred by the gospel. I have felt the story of Christ so strongly that I wept at seeing the great columns reaching out from St. Peter's in Rome, as if to encircle the entire world with God's love.

I have also felt it in equal strength in New Guinea, when one of our air crews belly-landed in a swamp three hundred miles from safety in the meanest jungle on earth. It was during World War II, and they had been shot down. The five young men scrambled from their aircraft as it slowly settled in the ooze. They sat on the wing, contemplating the fact that they could not survive so long a trek to safety. When they were almost crushed by despair, a solitary New Guinea warrior paddled up in his canoe, wearing a loincloth and sporting a human bone as an ornament. He was smiling broadly, waving to attract their attention and singing "Jesus Loves Me" in pidgin English. Long-John Manjohn had became a Christian, and although he was a while maturing completely out of the headhunting business, he finally became a stalwart member of the Pacific church. He saved the lives of my airmen friends, who insisted ever after that the short, stumpy, battle-scarred black man was the most handsome fellow they had ever seen. Also a world-class gospel singer!

There is a sequel to that story. When I was in Sydney, Australia, a few years ago, I discovered that Campbell Manjohn, Long-John's son, was in the city. We had dinner one evening, and I found that he has been working as a missionary from New Guinea to Australia. He has established two congregations that have become self-sustaining, but he has never drawn a salary from either. Campbell supports himself by teaching microbiology at one of the universities. His has been a saga almost beyond belief. He has gone from a headhunting society to a university campus in one generation, and I get the distinct impression that this would not have occurred except for the church. Campbell's father, Long-John, certainly had a vision of service for his children that was as great a leap as any parent anywhere. As with the African church, the Pacific church has exploded in growth and influence.

When I was interviewing the ministers for this book, I had a late-night meeting with two of them in a local restaurant. We had pie and coffee or tea and I mainly listened as they talked. Finally one of the ministers became curious about my position as we talked about the divisions that sometimes keep Christians and churches from fellowshiping as they might.

I told Jeffery Langston that I was an evangelical, or relational, Christian who believed that a personal commitment to Christ was best expressed through strong social action. It is my belief, I told the two pastors, that I have very little that can be donated directly to God. Everything I do for Christ must be cycled through other men and women in some way.

Jeff smiled and asked whether I was looking for a new church home. He had found, he went on to say, that social-action evangelicals are the best kind of members to have in his parish. He quipped that they are not only good; they are good for some meaningful spiritual purposes. Andrew, the other pastor, nodded and spoke about his large successful Lutheran congregation: "If I could get more of my people to see the best kind of Christianity as a synthesis of faith *and* works, we would be twice as effective as we now are."

We begin to meet our spiritual obligations as Christ's disciples most effectively when we begin to risk something for God. The parish may be a place for quiet meditation and contemplation at times, but it is also a battleground in which people are being crippled or destroyed unless led wisely. We can serve best in the church of the twentieth century by creating a community of faith, hope, and love that reaches out through salvation, social action, and self-help—the timeless foundation stones of Christianity.

As ministers of Christ, we must use sound concepts from a variety of sources to build better, more helpful congregations through which to reach our communities for Christ. We need sound acoustical, air-conditioning, and engineering experts as a congregation expands to larger buildings. We need professional help from time to time in order to finance programs and train church-school teachers. And we need to manage interpersonal relationships better, which I see as the reverse side of the leadership coin. By learning how and why people will or will not commit themselves to God, the church, and a vital leader, you can be in the best possible situation to turn a parish into a change agent—into the leaven in the loaf of life that Jesus spoke of so eloquently. Use all the ideas presented in this book and discover for yourself how valuable they are in your ministry for Christ *and* in your career.

Conclusion

I do not believe that you can build a great church by accident. To excel as a leader, you must use sound interpersonal relationships to develop a healthy congregation that worships, works, loves, learns and perseveres together. To sum it all up, you must strive for increasing excellence in three aspects of sound communal Christianity.

Spiritual Significance. A church can be considered great when it enables its people to live with a meaningful sense of spiritual significance. A great congregation shows its men, women, and young people that they are important in God's scheme of things. They realize that their lives do count for something for God, for others, and for themselves.

Arthur Miller, in his painful but perceptive play *Death of a Salesman,* addressed the insignificance felt by so many people today. During one of the recurring family conflicts, Willy Loman's wife told her son, "Be kind to him. He is only a small boat in a big harbor."

We all look for grand experiences and great people to help us feel significant. It has even been suggested that while no one wants war, almost everyone follows the band and marches in the parade because it "gives significance to little lives." Jesus understood that we all have our strengths and weaknesses—that while we may have our heads in the stars, our feet remain in earth's mud. To build a great church, regardless of its size, teach your people the significance of what they do for God and others.

241

Christ-Centered Maturity and Relationships. A church can be considered great when it offers its members relationships with other people that reflect their relationship with God. A great church also strengthens lives and guides them toward emotional and spiritual maturity. Deeds speak louder than words in our relationships with God and the Lord Jesus Christ and with other people as well.

Every reputable psychologist admits that we form new behavioral patterns faster and better by acting in new ways rather than by thinking new thoughts and hoping our behavior will change. We can develop spiritual and psychological strength faster by doing spiritual things rather than by waiting and praying for greater spiritual enlightenment. We need to pray and meditate, of course, but that cannot be the end of it; but merely the beginning of new insights and relationships that enable other people and ourselves to grow in maturity.

A Fellowship of Redeemed Believers. Finally, a great church is one in which the members care for each other deeply. From the very beginning, the Christian church has been a fellowship of the redeemed. Members of the early church were so close at times that they shared their homes, money, and lives in common. Obviously, neither that church or ours today was perfect, else Paul would not have written so many letters dealing with its shortcomings. Despite the failings of those new churches, however, they were a fellowship of the forgiven. They knew that they were in Christ, and nothing was ever the same after that. Modern congregations can do no less, although our society is much more complex and we have to work with people in a more sophisticated way.

The responsibilities of a parish leader sound formidable— and indeed they are! Meeting the challenge you have already accepted requires a steadfast commitment to Christ, strength under adverse circumstances, a loving understanding of human needs, and even self-sacrifice. You must be a fearless captain, bold in decision making, knowledgeable in your comprehension of pertinent factors, yet honest in dealing with your own and others' emotions and wise in your counsel. Only as you are open to necessary change, and flexible in knowing which role to assume or which talents to enlist from within your membership, will you be successful in building a warmly enthusiastic membership.

Show your people the relevance of Christianity in today's complicated world—offer them a spiritually significant experience, the opportunity to grow stronger in many different ways, and the realization that they are bonded in a unity of believers. Your skill in handling interpersonal relationships will be a catalyst as you teach them—above all—to love each other as Christ loves them.

Index

Munger method, 29

Nice Guys Finish First, 55, 71, 156
nice guy triad, 157
Nielsen, Paul, 145
Niemöller, Martin, 212
Nixon, Richard, 77, 107
non-directive counseling, 148–52

On Becoming a Person, 181
Oswald, Lee Harvey, 61
outreach, flexibility in, 225–26

Parish, differences, 45–48;
   influence, 41–43; leadership,
   89–160; participation, 48–49;
   progression, 43–45
Pasadena College, 211
Pastoral-Care Counseling, 227
Pastoral, differences, 72; emphases,
   236; influence, 34; leadership, key
   factors, 35–38; leadership
   workshop, 21; nature of, 152,
   research, 21, 36
pattern-based conflicts, 80
pattern, beginnings, 72; different,
   70–78; shifts, 83; strengths and
   weaknesses, 78–80; and stress,
   82–85
Patterson, Will, 92–93
Paul (Saul of Tarsus), 15, 16, 39, 50,
   125, 156, 193, 199, 227, 242
Pavlov, Ivan, 190
perception, selective, 169–76
perceptual screen, 170
Personal Dynamics Institute, 71
personal interpretations, 171;
   motivation, 54–55
personality, organizer, 84, 85;
   patterns, 69–85; primary, 77; and
   relationships, 69–85
Peter, 108, 193, 199
Pitkin, Howard, 81, 101
pleasure/pain principle, 56
politics or relationships, 50–51
Pope John Paul II, 35
Pope Pius XI, 212
Pope Pius XII, 212

position power, 23
positive reinforcement, 228–31
potential problem analysis, 101;
   chart, 103
power/prestige principle, 57
power, relational, 50
precisely identifying problems, 96
prejudice, 172
preconceived notions, 172
problem analysis, 94–105; chart, 95;
   flow, 101; process, 89–105
problem-solving circle, 89;
   independence, 49, 51
psychological reciprocity, 161
Psychology of Leadership, 33
Psychology of Witnessing, 27, 28,
   181, 213, 214, 221, 226
psychological reciprocity, 161–67
purpose/permanence principle, 57

quid pro quo, 164

Reagan, President Ronald, 78, 141
reasons for change, 204
reciprocity, and leadership, 162–64;
   psychological, 161–67
reinforcement, 188; listening,
   180–83; power, 24
relational leadership, 21–85; power,
   50
relationships, 21–85, 89–152,
   155–207, 228–31
Religious Right, 35
resources, balancing with
   relationships, 34
response and maturity, 48
responsibility, member, 166–67, 213
rewards, activating process, 190–91;
   appropriate, 185–200, 223–24;
   and assimilation, 223; modifying
   behavior through, 188–90; rules
   for, 188
Richard the Lionhearted, 33
Rickenbacker, Eddie, 144
Rivers, Joan, 77, 123
Roberts, Oral, 66, 92, 203, 235
Roberts, Patti, 92
Robertson, Pat, 113, 203

DATE DUE

11/30/2010